To my wife Nancy for always saying yes to the impossible. To my mother Joan for always believing I could. To my father Robbie for modeling a leadership style worth following. And to Brent Rue who gave me the opportunity to try.

CONTENTS

REVOLUTIONARY LEADERSHIP

Building Momentum in Your Church
through the Synergy Cycle

TRI ROBINSON

ampelon
publishing

ISBN: 0-9748825-3-4

Printed in the United States of America

Requests for information should be addressed to:
Ampelon Publishing
6920 Jimmy Carter Blvd., Ste. 200
Norcross, GA 30071

To order other Ampelon Publishing products, visit us on the web at: www.ampelonpublishing.com

Cover & inside design: Lisa Dyches (www.cartwheelstudios.com)
Graphics: k33n media (www.k33n.com)

FOREWORD

How does one determine validity in leadership? In a world that measures validity in terms of results and secured power, this is not an easy question. As the scales drop from one's eyes through the power of the Holy Spirit, we seek a leadership somewhat different from the world's. It becomes a leadership that does not depreciate others. Rather, it values, enriches, and frees those with whom one works. It exudes a love and concern, recognizing that we are all trapped in the human condition. It is a leadership that responds to God's gift of grace, the eternal hope for mankind and the restorations of our institutions.

Within the pages of this book is a clear depiction of what effective leadership looks like. It calls for a vision that is dynamically communicated and has a strategy for accomplishment. There is an added quality present in the Christ model of leading. It identifies the latent God-given gifts and talents of those with whom one works. It affirms the divinity of the Spirit as detected in the human personality. It seeks to nurture and help others in their maturing process. It is a leadership that lifts people rather than one which represses and controls. This is servant leadership – revolutionary leadership in today's world!

By the continual metamorphosis of being conformed day after day through the indwelling of God's Spirit, the secular can move toward the Holy and our institutions can become more of God's Kingdom. In theological terms, this is the process of sanctification. The idealism of this position should not dissuade us. Our Lord calls us not to assure success in the eyes of the world, but to obedience and faithfulness to His eternal plan for our lives.

This book is a work that brings new understanding to biblical truths, truths that lead to authentic church growth.

F. Willard Robinson, Ed. D.
Former Principal, Beverly Hills High School
Beverly Hills, California

ACKNOWLEDGEMENTS

A person's leadership style develops over a lifetime of experiences. It is difficult to express my appreciation when there are so many who have played a crucial role in who I have become as a leader. I do want to thank my staff and leadership team at Vineyard Boise, who have been a testimony of devotion and Christ-likeness; therefore, giving me the confidence and credibility to speak these truths without reservation. I am so thankful for their unwavering dedication to accomplish the vision and work the Lord has set before us. I especially want to thank my secretary, Lori Thompson, for working so hard through the years to make me a success. To Chad Estes, my sincere thanks for sharing his gift of editing. And to Jason Chatraw, thank you for encouraging me to finally write the book that hopefully communicates the passion and principles I hold so dear.

Letting Go

Becoming a fully functional church

In 1995, I found myself in crisis. At the time, I didn't understand what I was going through and yet somehow I knew I was in trouble. I was sitting in the Salt Lake City airport waiting for a connection flight to go teach a group of pastors about how to grow their churches. I was doing many leadership seminars in those days because our work in Boise, Idaho, had experienced rapid church growth in its first six years.

In 1989, my wife Nancy and I had led a church planting team of 12 families from the Desert Vineyard Christian Fellowship in Lancaster, California, to Boise to begin a new work. Our timing had been perfect. Boise was on the cusp of a surge of growth both physically and economically; and the area was ripe for a new church, contemporary in style and yet theologically balanced. The Vineyard met a need for many Christian families who were moving into the area, and, from the beginning, the church experienced steady continual growth. In the first four years, we changed facilities four times. In the first two months of existence, we moved from a small office complex to a little community church. Only a year and a half later, we were overflowing three services and were forced to consider our next building – an old super-mart that we completely remodeled. This facility proved to be inadequate only two years later. From there we purchased 22 acres and began building what would become the campus that serves the Vineyard Boise today. As I sat there pondering all of this, I realized what a whirlwind it had been – and to be honest, I had become weary.

From all appearances, the Vineyard Boise was doing very well for the most part; yet I was becoming dissatisfied and disillusioned. Somehow, it wasn't developing into the church I had dreamed of – a church where lives were being transformed because of the power of the Gospel and people were joining hands to accomplish great things for the sake of the Kingdom of God. In my mind, our Vineyard had become much like the cartoon character I remembered from my childhood known as "Baby Huey."

Baby Huey was a duck born fully grown. Because of his physical size and maturity level, it caused him and his parents unending trouble. That was exactly how I felt. We were experiencing major growing pains and I didn't really know what to do about it.

Growing pains can be dangerous because they can damage the

culture of the church, and one thing we will learn in the p
come is that culture is one of the most important elements in a
healthy church. Growing pains have a tendency to leak out in
phrases like, "This church is just getting too big," or "Nobody
knows my name," or "There's no place for me here anymore."
Growing pains can be detected in actions. For example, when
there seems to be a decline in the participation or enthusiasm for
worship or it becomes a drudgery to motivate workers for the
children's ministry or other essential ministries, a church may be
experiencing the strain of growing pains.

Because I fully believe the church is God's agency to fulfill His
great commission on earth, my passionate dream is to build a
church that produces mature and authentic Christians. I was not
convinced we were doing this. And the dilemma was that I was
traveling to meet a group of pastors to tell them how to do something I wasn't even sure I had the answers for myself.

While I sat there waiting in the terminal, I began a conversation with the Lord. In my state of self-pity, my communication
was primarily one-sided grumbling. (Especially those of you in
leadership may be able to identify with prayers like mine.) The
conversation went something like this: "Lord, I'm a lousy pastor
and I don't know what I'm doing. Why did You call me to do
something I don't know how to do? Lord, am I hopeless or is
there any help for a loser like me?" I'll be the first to admit that

it was a pathetic prayer, and I'm embarrassed to say that it went on like that for quite a while until I happened to glance down at the magazine that was sitting on the briefcase in front of me. I don't remember the name of the magazine, but the title of the feature article was what struck a cord: "Teamwork – A Leadership Style for a New Millennium."

What happened next is difficult to convey, but in retrospect, I realize that moment was one of the most pivotal in my life. The solution to my frustrations and the answers to everything I was asking came into focus. I realized that it was time for me to change my role. The reality hit me that I had been a player-coach on the team I had built, but now it was time to resign my role as a player and simply be the coach. My new job would be to build others up and empower them to play instead of trying to be the key player myself. My fulfillment and satisfaction as a leader would no longer come from throwing the winning touchdown pass, but rather from watching the people succeed that I coached. I was to become a trainer, an inspirational leader and a coach, organizing and challenging my team to achieve the great victory I sincerely believed God put before us.

> My new job would be to build others up and empower them to play instead of trying to be the key player myself.

In the mid 1980s, Bobby Clinton, head of leadership development at Fuller Seminary, challenged me to read a book called *How to Make the Transition from an Entrepreneur to a Professionally Managed Firm* by Eric G. Flamholtz. To be honest, I didn't even know what an entrepreneur was in those days. But of all the leadership books I've ever read (and there are many), this book helped more at this time than any other. The book is long since out of print (However, it has been reissued under the title *Growing Pains: Transitioning from an Entrepreneurship to a Professionally Managed Firm*) and I've loaned it out so many times I've often lost track of it; however, I will never forget the basic principles.

What I learned was that our church was much like an entrepreneurship and I was the entrepreneur. An entrepreneur is the founding leader of a developing organization. If a new business venture is going to make it through its developmental phase, it is largely dependent upon the energy and skill level of this primary leader and the team he assembles. Often it runs on the leader's dreams and charismatic gifting. Because entrepreneurs believe in what they are doing, they are willing to work 24 hours a day to see it happen. They have the ability to excite and motivate the people around them who respond by making sacrifices for the same dream. The problem with an entrepreneurship is that the organization can only go as far as this one key leader can take it.

Flamholtz's book convinced me that the only hope for a new venture to develop into a functional, thriving and fruitful organization hinges on the leader's ability to transition it into a "well-managed organization." It also enlightened me to the fact that the very makeup of the leader that makes him successful in the early phases of the organization can later become his demise when it is time to turn the management over to others who have better organizational skills.

Translated into church terminology – the body of Christ needs "bones" or structure in order to be fully functional. The church needs an army of well-trained and equipped saints who are willing to work together in harmony and unity for a common cause. I realized that the church is truly a living body that wants to mature, but in order to do so it must be in a constant state of change. I learned that healthy church growth requires a structure that will continually facilitate transition. It requires a senior pastor who is willing to give up the controlling entrepreneurial spirit and give away authority and responsibility to competent, willing people. What I discovered that day, while sitting in an airport terminal, led me to a new kind of leadership, a revolutionary leadership style that understands synergy and its three key components. In this book, we are going to explore these components and learn how to implement them in a way that can transform your church and energize the vision God has given you.

Beginning a Revolution
Understanding the
Principles of Transformation

Imagine the possibilities of what can happen when God begins to transform a community. It is infinite what God can do when His people are both individually and corporately devoted to following Him. For me, the endless possibilities started with a deflated helium balloon.

In the early spring of 1987, Michael Anderson was 12 years old. He stood on the front lawn of his church in Ontario, Oregon, holding a yellow, helium-filled balloon prepared earlier that morning in his Sunday School class. Inside the balloon, he had inserted a scrap of notebook paper with the handwritten words, "Let us love one another – 1 John 4:7 & 8." He released his balloon along with the rest of the class. It slowly rose into the cold morning air, drifting eastward with the prevailing wind toward the Idaho border.

A little over a year later in the summer of 1988, the last thing on my mind was planting a church in Idaho. My wife, Nancy, and

I were happily situated in a growing Vineyard church in Southern California. We felt secure and fulfilled in our ministry as associate pastors at the Desert Vineyard Christian Fellowship in Lancaster, California.

Nancy and I fell in love 20 years earlier when we met as students at the College of Idaho (now Albertson College) in Caldwell, Idaho. We married in 1970 and remained in Caldwell as newlyweds for two more years before moving to the mountains of California to raise our children on my family's ranch. I went to work as a schoolteacher for several years before joining the church staff in Lancaster.

In 1988, we received a phone call from an old Idaho friend. Pat Armstrong, who had remained close with Nancy and me since our college days, made his living building backcountry trails with a team of mules. We had often spent several of our summer breaks working for Pat while I was still teaching school.

At the time I received Pat's phone call, we hadn't worked for him in several years due to our responsibilities at the church. However, he called to ask for help on a project to reconstruct a damaged airstrip on the Middle Fork of the Salmon River. With a couple of weeks of vacation, we jumped at the opportunity and headed 800 miles north to Idaho. Our kids, Kate and Brooke, had heard many stories about our early days in Idaho but had never visited the state themselves. We were all content with our lifestyle on the family ranch. None of us had even considered leaving our comfortable California lifestyle – that is, until we passed through Boise on our way to meet Pat.

Vision never announces its coming, but when it comes, you know it. And before I knew it, vision was on my front porch, knocking loudly on the door.

I can't explain what happened that day, but I believe it was supernatural – our whole family fell in love with the city. God was definitely doing something in all of our hearts, but I was the last to admit it. Privately, Nancy asked me if I would ever consider giving up our life in California to plant a Vineyard church in Boise. Suddenly, fear began to stir in me because I had witnessed so many church plant failures. Without much thought, I defiantly answered, "No!" And I informed her that I didn't want to talk about it again.

Vision never announces its coming, but when it comes, you know it.

Two days later, we flew into Pat's camp on Mahoney Creek. Everyone was enjoying the time in the wilderness, except me. I was miserable. For many years, I had waited to get back to the mountains of Idaho, but I was not enjoying it. The thought of leaving the security of my established life really bothered me.

Leaving the ranch, risking everything, transplanting our family to an unknown place with no friends – it all seemed totally crazy and impractical.

Noticing my struggle, Nancy suggested that I take a long walk and get alone with God. Because of my attitude, I perceived her as really saying, "Why don't you take a hike?" Climbing a tall mountain adjacent to Mahoney Creek, I only stopped to catch my breath and pray. At one point, I remember crying out to God for an answer.

"Lord," I said, "I desperately need a word from you." But every time I stopped hiking, I never heard His voice. Then I figured God would speak to me once I made it to the summit, just as He spoke to Moses on Mt. Sinai. But His voice was absolutely quiet. Finally, I decided to stop guessing how God would speak to me and just enjoy the time I had in the backcountry with my family and friends.

As I began walking down an aspen-covered ridge, something caught my eye on the opposite side of the ravine. The bright yellow object looked out of place for the colors on the mountain terrain. Intrigued by this object, I ventured closer to see what it was.

I descended the ravine and scrambled up the opposite side. After climbing under a thorny berry bush, I emerged carrying Michael Anderson's deflated yellow balloon with an illustration of Noah's ark printed on the side. I sensed this particular balloon had been sent to me from the Lord and that it contained a message in it from Him. I felt the balloon and there was a small note inside. At first, I was almost afraid to remove it. I climbed back up the side of the ravine to a bright sunny spot and sat down. I ripped a small hole on the side of the balloon to remove the paper.

Here I was, sitting on a mountainside in the very center of the largest wilderness area in the continental United States. I had prayed all day for a word from God. As you can guess, the note read, "Let us love one another – 1 John 4:7 & 8." Oddly enough, at the time I remember telling the Lord that I needed a real word, a more specific answer to my question.

It was then that the Lord spoke to me through the Holy Spirit more clearly than I had ever heard Him before. He said, "Tri, I don't care where you do it. All I want you to do is build a church that loves people." Then He asked me, "Do you want to do it in Boise, Idaho?" It was at that moment that I discovered what He had already put in my heart. Without hesitating, I replied, "Yes, Lord, I do."

Later that morning, I wandered back into our camp at Mahoney Creek and found Nancy by the fire. She asked me if I had heard anything from the Lord. I pulled the balloon and small strip of notebook paper from my pocket, telling her that God had written me a note.

Confirmation to Continue

For someone who has been with Tri Robinson in all of his ministry endeavors, his wife Nancy has some stories to tell. But in all of their adventurous decisions, she knows that in each instance God was leading.

"What has been so reassuring to Tri and me all these years is that we knew that moving to Boise was God's idea; it certainly wasn't ours," Nancy said. "As we began moving into this process, we sensed that God was doing something. I even saw it in our children."

When she suggested he go pray about what God was doing in his heart while they were out in the Idaho wilderness, Nancy suspected God was stirring Tri's heart.

"I have been around Tri enough to know that when the Lord is giving him new vision, Tri needs time to hear from the Lord and work it out with Him," Nancy said. "When I told Tri that he needed to go figure out what the Lord was doing, he came home and shared how the Lord had spoken to him. I was really blessed and amazed at what God was doing."

The Lord continued confirming to the Robinsons His emerging plan for them to plant a church in Boise.

"God gave us a lot to stand on," Nancy recalled. "He spoke to our hearts many other times. The next winter after the Idaho trip, our family piled into our old 1951 Dodge pickup. We were driving home from a Christmas party at our neighbor's ranch and we had the radio on, singing along with the Christmas carols. Between our ranches, our old pickup truck picked up this station crystal clear, which was a miracle in itself because the pickup had trouble tuning in anything. Then we heard 'Merry Christmas and Happy New Year from Treasure Valley in Boise, Idaho.' We were picking up a KBOI broadcast from Boise over 800 miles away. That was just more confirmation for our family.

"We needed to know that beyond a shadow of a doubt this was the Lord's idea! Situations came up that really tested us and stretched us, but we never doubted that moving out in faith was what God wanted us to do."

What God was giving me was a vision I couldn't accomplish on my own or even with just my family. I needed several others to journey with me and make this vision from God a reality in the city of Boise. It was almost one year to the day from finding the balloon that we found ourselves back in Boise with 13 other families from the Lancaster church. They, too, felt God's call to go plant a church in Boise that would love people. This team of people would have not been able to fulfill this vision had they gone out alone. But together, we were a collection of believers who trusted that God was going to help us accomplish the purpose He had set before us.

Today, Michael Anderson's balloon is framed on my office wall. I often look at that note and remember God's faithfulness and His very clear commission for us to build a church where people love one another.

On a recent autumn day I had a moment of nostalgia that filled my heart with gratitude. Like many pastors, I often get so focused on the daily responsibilities of running a church that I forget to reflect on the miracles that God has done.

It was a Wednesday and I had just been to the Barnabas Center, our benevolence and outreach facility on our campus. I considered everything I had just observed, ministry and activity in every corner of the facility. I was aware that even though it was mid-morning on a weekday, the food pantry had many volunteers serving and distributing food to numerous needy families. In an adjoining area medical volunteers were working in our free clinic that provided medical assistance to people who couldn't afford it. In the hallway interpreters were interacting with Spanish-speaking clients. There was a team using a fork lift, unloading and moving pallets of food that not only supplied our warehouse but over 25 other food pantries in the community as well. In an adjacent class-room, there were 26 young people being instructed and trained to be missionaries. They would soon be deployed as medics and midwives in poverty-stricken communities. Behind the Barnabas Center, other people were harvesting vegetables in a large garden that supplied the food pantry with fresh produce for the poor.

As I walked back to my office from the Barnabas Center, I paused for a moment on a grass embankment that borders our athletic fields. I took advantage of this vantage point for a quick look around. From my viewpoint, I observed how our elementary school teachers lovingly interacted with their students as they par-ticipated in an outside activity. I then turned to look at our main facility – a system of buildings that houses numerous groups every week as well as multiple services on Sundays.

Centered between the children's wing and the administra-tion/adult education wing is a large sanctuary, a youth chapel and a big lobby we lovingly refer to as "Heritage Hall." Heritage Hall is what you might call the living room of the church. It was designed with the idea that church would be an all-week event. The main purpose of the hall is a warm, welcoming place for anyone who wants to hang out. It has a beautiful fireplace, flanked by leather couches and chairs, a coffee bar, a bookstore, and bistro tables complete with plug-ins for computers and Internet access. Often, someone is softly playing the baby grand piano sitting in the corner.

Standing there, viewing this place called Vineyard Boise, it struck me what God can do with a group of people committed to a life of discipleship. I became overwhelmed as I thought about all those who flow through this place on a weekly basis, people who faithfully work in so many areas to bring healing to the broken and hurting, the hundreds of people it takes to lead discipleship groups, children's ministries, youth programs and Bible studies. I thought of those who usher and greet as well as those who serve in the coffee bar week after week. It is truly a busy place.

As I pondered all of this, it struck me how much had happened since that day, many years ago, when I stood on a mountainside in the Idaho wilderness clutching a small yellow balloon. Finding this balloon inspired a clear vision to go build a church that would love people in the name of Jesus. I believe the greatest miracle isn't the size of Vineyard Boise or even the amount of ministry that pours out of it. Instead, it is the miraculous way that God has gathered so many to one place who have captured His heart and desire to be used by Him. Somehow, Vineyard Boise had become a 22-acre campus that facilitates literally hundreds of volunteers who were dedicated to the vision of building a church that would "love people." Only God could have done such a thing.

As I stood there, I realized what an incredible testimony this church is to the power of a God-given vision, a vision that had miraculously become reality in our life at Vineyard Boise.

Throughout this book, we're going to hear some of the real-life stories of people serving in our church who have experienced this radical transformation first-hand. But churches that change lives don't just happen overnight. You can't plant a church and hope to see it grow to a thousand members in a year. Not only is that extremely unlikely, it's also dangerous. Without the proper structure in place, a church can become little more than a popular place to visit on Sundays.

Every church leader wants to see his church or ministry grow, not because they desire to have a big ministry, but because they want to impact more lives for the Kingdom of God. Our discussion throughout this book about vision, culture, and structure will help equip you to develop the momentum you need to fulfill the vision God has placed on your heart. I trust these words will not be just another book full of ideas but practical advice that will change the way you lead in ministry.

Beginning a Revolution

Understanding Synergy
and Leadership

Have you ever found yourself caught in an activity that started out small and then spontaneously grew into a whirlwind that seemed to have a life of its own? Those of us who were around during the Jesus Movement will never forget that feeling. We felt like we were part of a giant snowball rolling downhill experiencing the thrill of momentum as it grew in size and speed. There are few things as exhilarating as finding one's self in the midst of a genuine expression of ministry growing both in magnitude and effectiveness. During the 1970's we called experiences like this "Holy Spirit happenings" and we never wanted them to end.

What I am describing is a phenomenon occurring as a result of synergy. Too often Christians experience synergy more by accident than on purpose. After personally experiencing the thrill and power of synergy, I began to ask questions: Is synergy a commodity that we can harness? Can we purposely lead our people into the power of this momentum? If the answers to these questions are "yes," which I believe they are, I propose that synergy is the catalyst for spontaneous church growth.

In the early days of the Vineyard movement I accepted a staff position at the Desert Vineyard to help organize and develop a number of struggling ministries. I had been a public educator prior to this role and had experienced the impact of synergy even in the classroom setting. Several times during my teaching career I felt the thrill of synergy as I led my students into creative projects that grew into nationally recognized events. Although these activities occurred in a secular setting and had different dynamics than happen in a spiritual arena, I knew some of the principles could be transferred into ministry. I also found this phenomenon had occurred in Scripture, especially in the early church as it is recorded in Acts.

When I began working at the church in Lancaster, my normal routine was to arrive early in order to have an hour of solitude before things got crazy in our office. Day after day I read Acts to see if I could discover what caused the first church to have the life and excitement it clearly possessed. I wanted to know if man could play any part in spontaneous church growth or if it was simply and completely an act of the Holy Spirit. My findings convinced me that although the church in Jerusalem was clearly birthed by the Holy Spirit in Acts 2, leadership played an important and significant role in its ultimate effectiveness. I discovered three important elements that I believe are the keys to the momentum of synergy: vision, culture, and structure.

Synergy is defined as *the action of two or more substances or organisms that together are capable of achieving an effect or result, of which each part is individually incapable of producing.*

What is impossible to obtain with *independence* can only occur when these substances come together and interact *interdependently*. One substance is ineffective without the presence and influence of the others.

Synergy is defined as the action of two or more substances or organisms that together are capable of achieving an effect or result, of which each part is individually incapable of producing.

The first century church had clear vision. They knew exactly what Jesus had commissioned them to do. Before His ascension, Jesus gave His small band of followers these clear instructions:

And he said, "Yes, it was written long ago that the Messiah must suffer and die and rise again from the dead on the third day. With my authority, take this message of repentance to all the nations, beginning in Jerusalem: 'There is forgiveness of sins for all who turn to

You are witnesses of all these things. "And now I will send the ⸻y Spirit, just as my Father promised. But stay here in the city until the Holy Spirit comes and fills you with power from heaven."

— L U K E   2 4 : 4 6 - 4 9

UNDERSTANDING TRUE VISION

True vision for the Church is most effective when we are certain it has come from God. Through the years I have seen many leaders become frustrated with the lack of growth or effectiveness in their church. What often happens is these leaders try to impose someone else's vision on the people God has entrusted to them to lead. This often creates more frustration, compounding the roadblocks to church growth. Instead of giving people a true vision from God for their church, frustrated leaders copy a program or system from a successful church or ministry. Now this vision may have been inspired by the Holy Spirit for a pastor at his megachurch, but that doesn't mean God meant it to be transferred to all churches in all communities and settings.

Jesus' disciples knew exactly what they were to do and obeyed. After Peter preached the Holy Spirit-inspired message on the day of Pentecost an amazing thing happened – people responded to the Gospel and gathered around it. He preached exactly what Jesus had told him concerning the resurrection, repentance and the forgiveness of sin. Also in obedience, he preached the message first in Jerusalem. There was immediate response to the God-given vision, and the first church was established and gathered into fellowship. As a result of a people gathering around this vision, a culture emerged that was alive and exciting.

They joined with the other believers and devoted themselves to the apostles' teaching and fellowship, sharing in the Lord's Supper and in prayer. A deep sense of awe came over them all, and the apostles performed many miraculous signs and wonders. And all the believers met together constantly and shared everything they had. They sold their possessions and shared the proceeds with those in need. They worshiped together at the Temple each day, met in homes for the Lord's Supper, and shared their meals with great joy and generosity – all the while praising God and enjoying the goodwill of all the people. And each day the Lord added to their group those who were being saved.

– A C T S   2 : 4 2 - 4 7

Why was the early church so successful? People rallied around a God-given vision and a thriving culture emerged that became attractive to the people who observed it from outside. Like that giant snowball, others were drawn into the church and it continued to grow in size and intensity.

I have always believed that church culture is a better vehicle for evangelism than an evangelism program. If people in a church are personally experiencing transforming change, they will tell their friends and invite them to share in the excitement. The problem with church growth is that it attracts more people, and people cause problems! Vision alone cannot sustain a movement of God. But synergy seamlessly melds vision together with culture and structure to produce a living organism that can excel in its purpose, achieving a high level of effectiveness when functioning properly.

TURNING VISION INTO REALITY

Many pastors and leaders do gain a true vision for their church from God but they struggle to turn the vision into reality. These leaders may have experienced God moving in incredible ways throughout their church. But instead of helping facilitate that move of God with appropriate structure, it fizzles out with little more than a moment of momentum. People fear that by building structure they will quench what God is doing. I believe the opposite is true. If structure is not added to what God starts, the powerful momentum can be short lived.

Again we can turn to Acts for an example. While pastors love to talk about having an Acts 2 church, the truth of the matter is the early church was on the fast track toward trouble until proper structure was added.

But as the believers rapidly multiplied, there were rumblings of discontent. Those who spoke Greek complained against those who spoke Hebrew, saying that their widows were being discriminated against in the daily distribution of food. So the Twelve called a meeting of all the believers. "We apostles should spend our time preaching and teaching the word of God, not administering a food program," they said. "Now look around among yourselves, brothers, and select seven men who are well respected and are full of the Holy Spirit and wisdom. We will put them in charge of this business. Then we can spend our time in prayer and preaching and teaching the word."

– A C T S   6 : 1 - 4

For the first time solid structure for ministry was built into the early church. Did this make a difference? Luke explains what happened next:

God's message was preached in ever-widening circles. The number of believers greatly increased in Jerusalem, and many of the Jewish priests were converted too.

– A C T S   6 : 7

A solid structure led to a much deeper impact on the community. The Gospel penetrated the hearts and souls of people deeper into Jerusalem. Suddenly, this wasn't just a good idea involving a few people; this was progress. God was at work and He was giving His leaders strategy on how to facilitate the moving of His Spirit.

Here is a diagram of what synergy looks like within a church:

In my mind I liken the concept of synergy with the Mazda rotary engine. If you drive a relatively new Mazda, your engine embodies this concept of synergy. When Mazda rolled out the rotary engine a few years ago, it demonstrated how an engine can be more powerful and more efficient.

Most cars contain a traditional four-stroke piston engine, where each cylinder has four tasks to make the engine turn: intake, compression, combustion, and exhaust. However, Mazda's rotary engine places each one of these tasks into a different section of the engine, allowing these tasks to be performed individually. With the smooth running rotary engine, vibration is reduced, revolutions are increased, and the engine runs much more efficiently. As a result, it can produce as much power in a smaller amount of space as a larger traditional engine.

Through the years, the rotary engine has undergone many refinements. But what has emerged has been an extremely efficient engine. As long as the spark plugs fired sequentially, firing one right after another in the right order, the engine moved. The faster the plugs fired, the faster the engine moved. The same concept is true with synergy – the right elements need to fire in the right order for the church to gain momentum and continue moving forward.

Understanding this power of synergy within the context of ministry is a primary way to elevate the effectiveness of your church. By studying this concept and applying it to the people you lead – whether it is a small church, a large church, or a ministry within a church – you can transform a ministry into a powerful tool for the Kingdom of God. Each segment of synergy is interdependent upon the next. If you have the power of synergy at work, you can empower the vision God has placed in your heart for your church and impact your community.

God-Given Vision
Igniting the
Synergy Cycle

W illiam could see the need around him. As he surveyed just
how needy the people were in the slums of London, he
realized there was only one thing he could do, one thing he was
compelled to do: share the love of Christ with the people on the
street. If William was seeking to win a popularity contest with the
religious powers of the city, he went about it the wrong way.
Pouring his life out to the "thieves, prostitutes, gamblers and
drunkards" who wandered the London streets was the only way
William saw to walk out his faith. But it didn't just stop with sharing Christ with them — William saw the need to disciple these
men and women, imploring them to do unto others as had been
done unto them.

Riding on a train one day, William had a powerful vision of
the lost, which he recorded on paper:

*I saw a dark and stormy ocean. Over it the black clouds
hung heavily; through them every now and then vivid light-*

ning flashed and loud thunder rolled, while the winds moaned, and the waves rose and foamed, towered and broke, only to rise and foam, tower and break again.

In that ocean I thought I saw myriads of poor human beings plunging and floating, shouting and shrieking, cursing and struggling and drowning; and as they cursed and screamed they rose and shrieked again, and then some sank to rise no more.

And I saw out of this dark angry ocean, a mighty rock that rose up with its summit towering high above the black clouds that overhung the stormy sea. And all around the base of this great rock, I saw a vast platform. Onto this platform, I saw with delight a number of the poor, struggling, drowning wretches continually climbing out of the angry ocean. And I saw that a few of those who were already safe on the platform were helping the poor creatures still in the angry waters to reach the place of safety.

William's vision also contained portions of unengaged Christians, standing on the platform, unaware that people were perishing around them. That image drove William to train and equip men and women to reach down from their "platforms" and pull people to safety.

However, moving a vision forward oftentimes meets great

resistance before any momentum is gained. For William, this was the case. His vision was to introduce the street people to Christ and connect them with a local church which could carry out the necessary discipleship. But because of the former behavior of many of these new believers, the church rejected them. William was back where he started.

So, William decided that if the church wouldn't accept these people, he would simply disciple them himself, hoping to train them up so they could do what he was doing with others. Within two years of hitting the streets, William had converted and equipped 10 people, who dedicated their lives to serving the street people. Within 10 years, William had released over 1,000 people to do the same work he was doing. William's vision from the Lord was clear.

In 1878 while proofing an annual report of his organization's activities, William noticed some peculiar phrasing, "the Christian Mission under the (sic) Superintendent's of the Rev. William Booth is a volunteer army." In one fell swoop of the pen, William crossed out the words "volunteer army" and replaced them with the words "Salvation Army." Later that year, the Salvation Army, under the direction of William Booth, refined its vision to person-ify its new name. Almost 100 years after Booth's death, the Salvation Army's impact is felt in every corner of the globe, assist-ing millions of people each year through their hardships while presenting the Gospel in a practical way.

ACQUIRING A VISION

Within Christianity, we enjoy our labels. By labeling people with a specific denomination, we understand where they fit on our spiritual grid. This behavior can seriously hamper our ability to obtain unity while attempting to confine people to a certain subset of beliefs and doctrines. The same can be said of leadership. Many people try to label leaders as well. Are you a visionary leader? Are you a quiet leader? Are you an administrative leader? People often limit leaders to a specific style of leadership, not leaving room for the leader to be well-rounded with several traits.

When it comes to vision, a strong distinction is made in leadership thought between structural leaders and visionary leaders. While there are certain elements that stand out in a particular leader's skill set, I believe every leader has the ability to be a complete leader; some simply are more naturally gifted than others. But leadership can also be a learned skill. You believe this too, or you wouldn't be reading this book!

I firmly believe every leader in ministry has a component of vision within his or her skill set. It is impossible to lead without vision. There must be an objective or goal you are working with others to achieve. If there is no goal, you are not leading with purpose; you are merely pointing the direction for a quick ƒ frustration for all those who are following you.

Since the first sparkplug in the synergy engine is vision, a leader has to know exactly what he or she is purposing to do. And then that vision must be developed.

LEADERS FOLLOW VISION

When I came to Boise, I knew what I wanted to do. God gave me a vision for a church plant because it was something He desired to accomplish – and I wanted to be a part of that vision. God put a passion in me for building a church from the bottom up, cultivating the vision for a new discipling church. Because other people trusted Nancy and I, when we shared this vision with others, there were a handful of families who followed us to Idaho. They joined us in pursuing the vision because they also believed it was God's idea and the right thing for them to do.

There seems to be this common idea concerning vision that says, "People always follow vision." But I don't believe this is necessarily the case. Instead, I believe it is leaders who follow vision. Leaders smell vision. And if they find authentic vision, they recognize it is too big to accomplish alone. When given the prospect of contributing to something significant, people follow vision-driven leaders. Emerging leaders want to be around vision-driven leaders who will release them and allow them to exercise their own gifts and abilities. Leaders who possess authentic vision are able to gather other leaders.

Many times pastors will go to seminars and conferences looking for tools for their own ministries. They visit successful churches with the hope of finding the key ingredients they may be lacking. But oftentimes what happens is they try to bring those successful churches' programs back to their church and implement them exactly as they were presented. Instead of bringing back vision, the pastor has brought back another program. Those leaders weren't really inspired by God's vision for them; it was the fruit of programs from other churches that was so appealing.

As a leader, you have to go to the Lord and discover the one thing God has put in your heart. You have to discover the thing that will get you up every morning and over the rocky years and seasons of ministry. You have to believe in this vision so strongly that you will still hold to it no matter how much resistance you meet. That's why I have the yellow balloon hanging in my office. When things are difficult, I look at that balloon and say, "But, God, you told me to do this." The message to "go love people" is really the foundation of discipleship that we envisioned to the people of our church. That's what gets me up every morning!

When you possess that vision, what you really have is divine focus. If it's authentic vision, it is easier to communicate because you understand it and have passion for it. When leaders don't have authentic vision, they have a tendency to confuse people.

NEHEMIAH: A VISION FOR RESTORATION

One of the great examples regarding God-given vision is in the book of Nehemiah. I taught this Old Testament book to our young church plant in Boise. His story is one of my favorites because Nehemiah was a regular guy. He was a cupbearer, a servant, to Artaxererxes, the King of Persia. Although he had no real authority in his position, God started something special in his heart when his brother Hanani and other men visited from his homeland.

Anxious to hear about the condition of Jerusalem and his native people, Nehemiah asked the visitors for a report. He received an unfavorable response and responded with grief and heartache.

They said to me, "Things are not going well for those who returned to the province of Judah. They are in great trouble and disgrace. The wall of Jerusalem has been torn down, and the gates have been burned." When I heard this, I sat down and wept. In fact, for days I mourned, fasted, and prayed to the God of heaven.

– NEHEMIAH 1:3-4

Here we see Nehemiah far from home when his heart becomes broken for the people of Jerusalem. Nehemiah launches into this major prayer of intercession because he didn't know what to do. In this moment, God began to birth a vision in Nehemiah.

When people ask me if vision is "natural" or "supernatural," I answer, "Yes." Vision is comprised of both the natural and the supernatural. Nehemiah knew the condition of Jerusalem. Some scholars suggest that he had been to Jerusalem in an earlier time and returned. No one knows for sure, but the idea rings true that Jewish people living in Persia were constantly asking about how their homeland was and the condition of the people in it. So, Nehemiah had a natural component to his vision.

The same could be said for us. We know that our cities need help. We know there are drug problems, homelessness, crime, and brokenness. In the natural, we see the broken people of the world around us and we develop a heart for them. But still that is not enough to see the fullness of a God-given vision begin to take shape.

What also happened to Nehemiah in this moment of time – something leaders often experience – was that something supernatural happened in him. Somehow, he discovered what God had already placed in his heart – a deep passionate desire to see Jerusalem restored. So strong was this desire that it drove

Nehemiah into intercession. Real intercession happens when God breaks your heart for a certain situation and you are driven to cry out to Him in order to see transformation occur.

An "Impossible" Vision

While Nancy and I were living on a ranch that had been in our family for years, God stirred my heart to see the impossible happen. Our neighbor's ranch (which had originally been a cattle ranch owned by my grandfather) was being used for race horses. We had driven by their ranch gate dozens of times without a second thought. But one day as we passed by the gate, the Lord spoke to us.

At the time, I was a schoolteacher and not yet working in full-time ministry. However, I understood the vision of our church. I knew one of our desires was to have a place to train young people for the mission field. So, while I understood the need in the natural, the Lord now spoke clearly to us: "I want to build this school on your neighbor's ranch." And that was impossible.

What Nehemiah felt impressed to do was also impossible. For him to travel hundreds of miles to Jerusalem to rebuild the wall, *and* to have permission to do it, *and* to have the necessary resources was impossible. But that didn't stop his heart from breaking. This drove Nehemiah to fasting; it drove him to a point of mourning. Nehemiah began to intercede.

As a result of God speaking to Nancy and me about our neighbor's ranch, I experienced true intercession for one of the first times in my life. I couldn't sleep. I would get up and start walking the perimeter of my neighbor's ranch, laying my hands on their fence posts, praying and asking the Lord to give it to us. I prayed day and night for that place. No matter what I did, the desire to see this vision become a reality wouldn't go away.

Finally, I went to my pastor, Brent Rue, and said, "Hey, you want a ranch?"

"What for?" he asked.

"Well, to train young people to go into the nations," I answered.

Like all sharp pastors, he said, "Well, how much will it cost?"

And in a faith-filled visionary moment, I responded, "Well, if it's the Lord, it won't cost anything."

At that moment, I was talking completely based on my faith in God. I had no concept of how this could work. There had been no conversations with our neighbors. The idea that we were going to use their ranch to train missionaries was something that merely rested in my heart.

One afternoon before Christmas, I was stirred up because of the vision that had been churning in my heart. (It's moments like these when Nancy encourages me to go be alone with the Lord!)

I saddled up my horse as it began to snow and rode up the mountain to pray on this cold bitter day. I came into a clearing at the top of the mountain and happened to see Terry, the foreman of my neighbor's ranch.

"Terry, what are you doing up here?" I asked, stunned to see anybody on this remote part of the mountain on such a miserable day. She, too, was out riding, thinking about her problems.

"I've got a problem," she began. "The owners of the ranch are very discontent with us and the quarter horse business. They want us to keep up the entire ranch, and we just have an interest in the horses. We don't have the desire to keep up their big hacienda and all the other facilities and buildings on the ranch."

These buildings she referred to would be perfect for housing students. Also on the property was a building that could serve as a cafeteria, which had been built to feed the ranch hands and other workers.

Though it started as a miserable day, the light began to dawn in me. "Why don't I make you a deal?" I suggested. "You move down to the horse area to care for the horses, and Nancy and I will take care of the rest of the ranch."

"Why would you do that?" she asked.

"Well, I'm a nice guy," I said, partially moved out of compassion for Terry's predicament, mostly moved by the seed of vision God had planted in my heart.

After our discussion, Terry took my proposal to the owners of the ranch, explaining how we would keep up the property in exchange for permission to use the property to house and train our young people for missions. When I met Terry on the mountain, I had no idea that she or the owners were so desperate to change their state of affairs. This was something only the Lord knew and could orchestrate. Within two weeks, we had a five-year contract to take over a portion of the ranch. The church immediately began preparing it for a training school for young people. At the time of the writing of this book, that ranch is still operated by the church for ministry purposes.

In my heart, I realized the vision God gave Nancy and me was authentic vision. The most telling outward sign that a vision is God-given is the fact that it continues to run long after the visionary leader leaves. Years after I left for Idaho, the school continued to operate. Obviously, God was the author of this vision.

FROM INTERCESSION TO BIRTH OF A VISION

As Nehemiah ended his time of prayer and intercession, his final petition was that God would help him by granting him favor with his authority, King Artaxerxes. The next time Nehemiah came before the king, he was frightened. His job as the cupbearer was to bring joy to the king, but instead he went into the king's court with a despondent countenance. Though Nehemiah risked losing his head by expressing grief instead of joy in the king's presence, he could not hide the despair he felt in his heart for the people of Jerusalem.

The moment Nehemiah walked into his presence, King Artaxerxes recognized Nehemiah was suffering inner turmoil. Nehemiah quickly prayed for God's help, and God immediately gave him favor with the king. When prompted, Nehemiah expressed his heart to the king and shared his vision for the restoration of Jerusalem. The king asked him what Nehemiah would need to accomplish the vision. Nehemiah proceeded to give him a wish list – the king's blessing, the king's provision, and the king's protection. The king sent Nehemiah with everything he needed – an army, provisions, and a letter of authority. In this moment, it was noted that the queen was sitting by King Artaxerxes' side (an anomaly in those days) when he gave this authority to Nehemiah, which I believe is a statement that Nehemiah received all authority.

Once Nehemiah arrived in Jerusalem, he told no one that he was there. When our team moved to Boise to plant our church, we also didn't announce our presence. I didn't schedule a meeting with other religious leaders to tell them the Vineyard had arrived in Boise. In fact, I didn't even put a sign in front of the small office space we rented. We were surveying the situation until we sensed God moving us to begin the work of planting a church.

In the same manner Nehemiah scoped out the situation in Jerusalem, taking only his inner circle with him after an initial solo expedition. Under the cover of night, he took a handful of people with him to survey the walls. This is a picture of a strategic leader doing a demographics study, analyzing the situation before he casts the vision to the people. Nehemiah prepared a total description of the wall – what was burned down and what was torn down. He did all of this work before he unveiled the vision:

But now I said to them, "You know full well the tragedy of our city. It lies in ruins, and its gates are burned. Let us rebuild the wall of Jerusalem and rid ourselves of this disgrace!"

– NEHEMIAH 2:17

Nehemiah understood the key to effectively selling vision. A great leader comes before the people with a strategic plan. And as soon as you pull the trigger, you must be ready to execute. Forget the notion that some leaders are merely visionaries – if you can not articulate a plan to go along with the vision, you merely have an idea, not a functional vision.

Nehemiah continued his hard sell of this vision:

*I told them how the gracious hand of my God had been on me, and
what the king had said to me. They said, "Let's start rebuilding,"
and they were encouraged to [do] this good work.*

— NEHEMIAH 2:18, NASB

And the people began to do the "good work." This story has
a fascinating, almost unbelievable, ending. But it began with
Nehemiah understanding the necessary components to effectively communicate the vision God had placed in his heart.

SHARING VISION

In terms of breaking down how vision is effectively shared
with others, there are three major lessons we can learn from
Nehemiah:

1. **<u>Authentic vision is built around a need – and that need
must be shared.</u>** When Nehemiah stood in front of his potential
helpers, he essentially told them, "Look at the situation we're in!
Look at the mess we're in!" As a pastor or a leader in ministry, you
will have a difficult time advancing the vision God has given you
if you don't articulate the need with your people. For instance,
you can say to your church, "Look at the condition of the poor!"
But you only do that after you've analyzed the situation. You need
to have the numbers, you need to have the facts, you need to have

a plan; and then you sell your people on the reality of the situation in front of you. They may have an idea of the situation by what they can see – they have observed the poor man on the street corner. Your role is to come to them with more specific details that go to the core of the issue – why the poverty exists, the reaching effects of the poverty, and what your church can do to minister to the need.

The key phrase Nehemiah used in sharing the need is "let us." The minute I pull the trigger and sell the vision, it's no longer *my* vision. Now, it's *our* vision. If it's going to happen, we all have to own it. People may *follow* a visionary leader, but you really want people *believing* in the vision. The visionary is the person who brings organization and strategy to move the vision into action, but the people are the ones who own the vision and accomplish it. If the vision is authentic and compelling, they will want to participate as much as the visionary who had God's dream in the first place.

When I talk about Vineyard Boise, I don't say this is *my* church – it's *our* church. I had a vision for it, but the day I shared the vision with a group of people, it was no longer my own. I strongly feel that is one of the major reasons almost our entire church planting team has stayed with us all these years.

Catching the Vision

After serving overseas with Youth with a Mission (YWAM), Ruben Navarette returned to southern California and quickly became successful in real estate, land development, and foreign investment markets. Though he was no longer immersed in a mission-oriented environment, he still desired to serve in the local church. He began serving with a youth group led by Tri Robinson at the Desert Vineyard. Not long after that, the rumors began.

When Ruben confirmed the news, his heart sank: Tri and his wife were leaving Lancaster to plant a church in Boise, Idaho. With mixed emotions, Ruben pondered their departure.

"My initial thought when I heard Tri and Nancy were leaving was, 'I'm really going to miss them — they're such great people," Ruben says. "Tri was dynamic and a lot of fun to work with, something really critical when it comes to being on a team. You knew whatever he did was going to be exciting and adventurous. He had a history of doing exciting things."

Then God began to ever so slightly stir anticipation in Ruben's heart. But it came at a most unexpected moment, a moment when everything was smooth sailing.

"I was in the process of living my life," Ruben said. "I didn't have any plans of leaving southern California at the time. My professional life was doing well — I was driving a Mercedes. But then it literally happened out of the blue.

"I was on an airplane flying between St. Louis, Missouri, and Portland, Oregon, when the pilot said, 'If you'll look out your right-hand window, you'll see Boise, Idaho.' I started thinking about Boise being the place Tri and Nancy were moving to. It was at that moment that I heard the Lord say, 'I have plans for you there, too.' I thought about moving myself — and it was almost devastating to me. But then I thought, 'Well, if I was going to go with anybody, Tri is the guy to go with.'"

After meeting with Tri and telling him that he was pondering joining the church plant team, Ruben said things really began to stir in his heart. Taking some time off to pray about the issue, he finally gave Tri his answer.

"One key thing about Tri was that he never acted too excited," Ruben recalled. "Tri wanted each person or family's decision to be their own decision, not him pressuring them to go. But I took so long to give him my final answer that he finally asked me one day about my final decision."

Ruben affirmed his desire to take the plunge — and his heart began to experience transformation.

"In the process of saying 'yes' to God's call on my life to go be a part of this church plant in Boise, things began to change," Ruben said. "Tri brought me in and gave me a very clear vision of where we were going. With my background in finances, I worked on the church's incorporation procedures and worked through an attorney so we could start receiving donations.

"The vision Tri had was really well-defined and exciting, but God was moving so strongly on us when we first started meeting that I think whatever we did, God would have blessed it."

Though years have passed since the beginning phases of the church plant, the lessons Ruben learned after following God's lead in this adventure stick with him.

"It was one of the most exciting chapters in my entire life," Ruben said. "It was following God, being with a real leader and having a lot of confidence in Tri and what God was leading him to do. It was great to be with a guy who knows who he is and understands what God has called him to."

Nehemiah released his vision to the people by sharing with them what God had done in his heart. He wanted them to know about God's favor on his life to see this vision become a reality, not to brag and put up the pretense that he was super spiritual, but to let them know that restoring Jerusalem was not something he dreamed up on his own. This was God's vision.

> Nehemiah released his vision to the people by sharing with them what God had done in his heart.

During our class at Vineyard Boise that introduces people to our church, we always relate the story of the yellow balloon. I want them to know that the church was not my idea; it was God's idea. The balloon story actually reveals it wasn't my idea until God planted that suggestion in my heart. It never was a design of my own; our church was God's idea from day one.

2. **People must understand that the leader has been given authority to begin the work.** Nehemiah clearly communicated the fact that the Jewish remnant had the authority to rebuild the walls of Jerusalem. He made it explicitly clear that he was not riding into town merely fulfilling his own agenda. The king had given Nehemiah the authority to lead this venture.

It is very important, especially in church ministry, to understand from where this authority comes. I know it is significant to people in our church when I tell them that Vineyard Boise is under the authority of the Association of Vineyard Churches. It is also important that the people following me in ministry understand I am not a lone ranger. Starting at the very beginning, I had a pastor send me out to do this work of planting a church. We had authority, protection, and even provision from our sending church in Lancaster. We weren't independent people going on an independent journey.

> It is also important that the people following me in ministry understand that I am not a lone ranger.

The realization of where authority comes from helps instill confidence in people for their leader. If their leader is working within the confines of accountability, so can they.

3. Share your implementation plan for accomplishing the vision. I love how Nehemiah writes that the people immediately started to work once he shared the vision. People can be excited by a vision, but they quickly will grow frustrated if we have no framework to put around it. All momentum – and trust – you may have built up with those people will wane in the face of a vision lacking a clear plan and direction.

While working on staff at the Lancaster Vineyard, I met with our senior pastor, Brent Rue, for breakfast once a week. During our time together, we would discuss the health of the church and how things were going. He always asked me one specific question: "What hole is below the waterline?" That was his way of asking what was drawing life out of our church. At one of our meetings, it was clear what the biggest life-sucker was: the youth program. To be honest, it was a neglected ministry. But with my daughter in high school, I had a personal interest in helping the youth ministry succeed. So, I told Brent, "Our youth ministry really needs more help." And then he asked me to fix it.

I had been a junior high teacher for 12 years, and I thought I had paid my dues with youth! I couldn't duck fast enough when he pointed his finger at me, telling me that this ministry was now my responsibility to resurrect. With all the directionless wandering our youth had endured, I felt like they needed a ministry with a strong theme and good vision. So, I started praying for new vision for our youth ministry.

In those days, the Hard Rock Café was a popular restaurant in major U.S. cities, particularly in southern California. After praying and bantering around some ideas, we came up with the idea of turning our youth room into the "God Rock Café." We decided to build a type of Christian nightclub, but how to do it was the question. Our building was made of cinder block, a bare bones warehouse facility. The last place any teenager would want to go would be this building. It was cold and uninviting, a sure deterrent to growth. Not to mention that most youth group meetings consisted of some poor guy trying to coax the kids to sit in a circle while he played the guitar trying to get them to worship. It was a nightmare of a situation.

The first step in our plan was to build some tables to make the environment of our room more warm and inviting. I cut out the round table tops and drilled holes to connect the legs. However, I didn't assemble, paint, or finish the tables. We collected all the parts to build these tables and loaded them into my horse trailer.

At our next youth meeting, I shared the vision with the teens. I said, "Look at this building. Look at this room. Who would want to come to a youth group here? What we really need to do is turn this into a Christian nightclub and call it the 'God Rock Café!'"

Instead of getting a response from the people like Nehemiah, all I received was barely audible muttering, that went like this: "Yeah, yeah, right. We've heard that before." And they were right; they had heard things like this before. Many promises had been made to our youth, but they had been broken. Adult leaders had entered the doors of their youth room and told them they were going to do all these great things, but nothing ever happened. Now they weren't going to believe anything.

What happened next was important. I told them that we were going to build the God Rock Café and we were going to start right now. At this moment, our leadership team rolled up the garage door to our warehouse, backed in the horse trailer, and started unloading all of the table parts. Suddenly, the kids took interest. Instead of the murmuring, they said, "We've got to build these tables." We gave them the bolts, the stands, and the table tops – and they started the work.

Ten minutes after sharing the vision with the youth, they started building and painting tables. Immediately, we executed the plan, knowing we had to win them from the moment we cast the vision. We knew we wouldn't get another chance. The kids caught the vision and that began to turn the tide for the youth in our church and community.

Part of the genius of Nehemiah is that he started the work immediately. He did his homework, and then he began the work with the people. The third chapter of Nehemiah might appear to be a boring chapter, but it reveals the true genius behind Nehemiah's giftedness in the areas of administration and organization. He gave people jobs to do that matched the desires of their hearts. He told the priests to build the gate where the sacrifices entered the city because Nehemiah knew this was the most important section of the wall to them. He gave families in one particular part of the city the section of the wall that would protect their homes. The miracle of the massive wall restoration was that they accomplished the work in only 52 days, even while their enemies were coming against them.

Empowering Youth

When Casey Corum walked through the doors of the God Rock Café, he had no idea how his life was about to change. He was more interested in the young girl who had issued the invitation to him than in discovering a relationship with God. But even an unchurched teenager heading in the wrong direction couldn't avoid getting his heart captured by something much more beautiful: God's love.

The last time Casey had ever participated in a Christian youth setting, he left feeling empty and shallow.

"Even before I was a Christian, I believed that if God was real, then He's important," Casey said. "Surely, we can come up with better things to do than to sing parodies of 'Louie, Louie' and shuck corn with your feet, which is what kids did at some of the events I had attended. I thought, 'If this is what they believe God is about, then I don't want to be a part of this. It doesn't seem real. You shouldn't have to dress God up in a silly costume to make Him relevant.'

"Then I started dating this girl prior to visiting the God Rock Café," Casey said. "She told me that she needed to break up with me because I wasn't a Christian. I told her I was a Christian because I lived in America. We were still discussing our situation when I made the decision to go to church with her."

The moment Casey walked into the God Rock Café, he sensed a deep relevance in what was occurring, despite the fact that his focus was still on the girl who brought him.

"The packaging as the God Rock Café may have caused me to take a second look at what was going on, but what I saw beneath the surface was a group of high school kids in a reformed garage in an industrial park area, praising God and reaching out to Him," recalled Casey, who sported long hair and earrings at the time. "They were kids who looked like me. I wasn't your church poster boy. The God Rock Café had conservative preppy kids along with long-haired kids and punked-out kids from the subcultures of the 80s. They were kids like me who believed God was real, so much so that they could reach out to Him. The worship was led by youth; the teaching was led by youth, the ministry was done by youth. You weren't just like waiting to become an adult to have a real serious relationship with God; it could happen now."

Instead of simply creating a fun environment for the youth of the church, the God Rock Café became a place where kids connected with each other as well as God.

"Looking back on it now, I realize that God's presence was there," Casey said. "I wouldn't have used language like that at the time, but that's what it was. I went for a couple of weeks and then went to regular church service for the first time. The worship leaders took me aside and shared the Gospel with me. I actually joined the God Rock worship team right then. They needed a drummer, which says more about their need for a drummer than my ability to play the drums."

Through serving on the worship team at the God Rock Café, Casey forged a lasting relationship with Tri.

"I know that one of Tri's biggest goals was to empower the kids to lead and have ownership in this whole ministry," Casey said. "And that's really how it was. Ultimately, I think the God Rock Café allowed the youth to take God seriously and not have to wait to follow God. It was not just an adult thing. We realized you can follow God in your teens. He will use you no matter how old you are."

That was just the beginning for Casey, who still lives with the great expectation of what God will do next, something he learned in an exploding youth group. He eventually moved to Boise after the church plant was started and eventually became the worship leader. In 2003, Casey moved to Houston, Texas, to become the production director for Vineyard Music USA.

"Through being involved with that youth group, I learned that God had a purpose for my life that was eternally significant," Casey said. "He interrupted all my grand plans for life, and I'm so thankful He did."

Once the vision begins to build momentum, look out! Through acknowledging your God-given vision and desiring to lead others on a God-sized adventure, you will begin down an exciting path. But to be an effective leader once you have ignited a group of people and turned the vision over to a collective group, you must turn your attention toward engineering the culture that is emerging.

The Culture Component

Understanding How Culture Works

Before there was an information superhighway, getting information from one place to another was either extremely slow or extremely expensive. Communicating with someone could take days. Without cell phones, if people weren't near a telephone, they were inaccessible. Without e-mail, zipping a short message to someone took a week or so in the United States and much longer if sent overseas.

However, at the forefront of our cultural revolution in communication was a machine that had great potential for sending information: the fax machine. All the way back in 1843, an Englishman named Alexander Bain devised a machine that could reproduce writing on two electrically conductive surfaces linked together with a wire. However, this invention made no significant impact on the culture of communication.

After a handful of other inventions, German inventor Arthur

Korn developed telephotography, a method of breaking down photographs and transmitting them over electrical wires. In 1907, he transmitted the first inter-city fax from Munich to Berlin. But the vision for this invention stalled again. Nearly 60 years transpired before Xerox developed a fax machine that was easy to use and could connect to almost any telephone line. Still, it wasn't until many Japanese electronics manufacturers began producing inexpensive fax machines in the late 1970s did the momentum with fax machines begin, and it wasn't until the mid-1980s that the shift really picked up steam in the United States.

Over 150 years ago, there were people with a vision for transmitting images and documents electronically. But it wasn't until the electronics industry was able to make this vision accessible (inexpensive and easy to use) to the people that the culture shift took place.

BECOMING A CULTURAL ENGINEER

In the life of church leadership, having vision is not enough. Once you have established the God-given vision of the church with your leaders, the next component becomes vital to the degree to which the vision will become reality. That component is culture. As you begin to build upon the vision, a healthy culture must emerge in order for the vision to move forward. A great vision with an unhealthy culture will result in a glaring absence of sustained momentum. Like pushing an out-of-gas vehicle on a ¹ surface, you can begin to move the car forward with much effort; however, once the first hill appears, your own strength won't be enough to make it to the top.

Working with many churches throughout the years, I have observed that each one has a unique and distinct culture. Some churches have great cultures, which create healthy and maturing Christians. Other church have inadequate cultures that create immaturity that oftentimes results in a church split or closing. All churches have culture – the difference is whether it is life-giving or anemic.

> My primary role as a senior pastor is that of a cultural engineer.

My primary role as a senior pastor is that of cultural engineer. I am charged with the task of cultivating an atmosphere where people's lives can thrive. For instance, I want our staff to be growing in the calling God has placed upon their lives. I want the emerging leaders in our church to feel safe and nourished as they discover the passion God has placed within them. I want newcomers and new believers to experience God's love and compassion from other people in our church. None of these things happen in a church unless someone is committed to fostering a healthy atmosphere that allows these healthy behaviors to develop.

Church culture is an intangible that cannot be underestimated. For example, take evangelism. When we survey newcomers to find the reasons they began coming to our church, they do not typically identify the evangelism program of Vineyard Boise. Instead, they would say something like, "I came because somebody invited me and they were having a good experience in your church." In other words, positive church culture is a magnet. People who experience the love of Christ in our church and have a life-changing transformation tend to tell others about it. When people experience true life change, they can't keep quiet – and those people within their realms of influence are going to be invited to come visit the church for themselves.

Let's look back to Acts 2 to see how Luke describes the culture that was developed in the church after Pentecost:

They joined with the other believers and devoted themselves to the apostles' teaching and fellowship, sharing in the Lord's Supper and in prayer. A deep sense of awe came over them all, and the apostles performed many miraculous signs and wonders. And all the believers met together constantly and shared everything they had. They sold their possessions and shared the proceeds with those in need. They worshiped together at the Temple each day, met in homes for the Lord's Supper, and shared their meals with great joy and generosity – all the while praising God and enjoying the goodwill of all the people. And each day the Lord added to their group those who were being saved.

— ACTS 2:42-47

Many pastors read this passage looking for a formula for church growth. But we do not read that it was slick programming that helped the early church arrive at such dramatic life change Instead, these were the behaviors that were naturally emerging from the early church's culture. God was adding daily to their church. What was drawing them? It was the culture. You simply cannot get the same life out of a program that you get from a healthy culture.

Corporate culture begins when people gather together around a common cause or vision.

What was happening in Jerusalem was a revolution within that culture. People did not normally act the way Luke described. Consider the parable of the Good Samaritan as an example of how Jesus described the pious and legalistic attitudes of the religious leaders. They were more concerned with strictly abiding to the law than showing compassion to a dying soul. Suddenly, this new cultural shift led by Peter and the disciples shook the religious circles in a good way. Now, there was a new way to demonstrate love for God – a new way to enter into relationship with Him. Imagine the impact of this cultural shift of how to determine your religiosity. It had been based on being openly pious and legalistic, but now it was moving to being lovingly open to sharing the love of God with everyone.

Corporate culture begins when people gather together around a common cause or vision. In the first and most innocent stages, a leader says, "Let's go plant a church." Honestly, that's what gets people going in the first stages of church planting. Initially, that is good enough. But as time goes on, the leader needs to develop the vision into something more specific, such as, "Let's go make disciples."

SHAPING CULTURE

The notion that culture can be shaped is foreign to many leaders. They rightly assume a culture will develop in their church, but many leaders fail to take ownership of it. Unfortunately, an unhealthy culture can delay progress in a church for years. However, a good leader will be strategic in starting the culture and active in shaping it.

In its early stages, corporate culture promotes an attitude of positive expectation. Then as people connect the vision to momentum, the culture turns into a snowball rolling downhill. As a snowball progresses, it builds both size and speed. Your goal as a pastor is to make sure that the snowball doesn't break apart. You run out in front of the snowball to ensure that the pathway is clear. You remove any obstacles that might cause it damage. You must be forward thinking, looking down the road to prevent any hindrance that would cause the progress to lose momentum.

There is something powerful about momentum. If you've ever been involved in a movement where there was significant momentum, you understand the power behind it. In the early stages of a movement, there is something exciting about the prospect of what might become. As a pastor or leader, you must insure that the excitement and early momentum doesn't dwindle.

As a church begins to grow, the idea of spontaneity and creativity remains fresh in the minds of everyone involved. Nothing has become routine yet. Even the vision of what you're doing and what you're for has not solidified. It's still fluid—and there is something very exciting about that to people. And you really don't want to damage that if you can avoid doing so.

A CULTURE OF SERVING

In the early days of our church, we had a food pantry ministry, mainly because our church planting team needed food. We were relatively poor in those days. But with this ministry, we tried to help those outside of the church as well. As we continued to reach out, the ministry continued to grow, and with the growth came the need for more space.

While we were still in the embryonic stages of ministry to the poor, I began teaching through Matthew, delving into the story in Matthew 25 where Jesus told His disciples, "If you've done it unto the least of these, you've done it unto me." During the teaching, one of our men, Rocky Ketchum, became inspired. After hearing the message that Sunday morning, Rocky took his family to a local park for a picnic. It just so happened that his family sat down to eat at a place where many of the homeless in our city tend to stay.

While Rocky was grilling some food for his family, he and his wife Diane noticed some homeless men nearby and began talking about the implications of the teaching from that morning. Rocky looked at Diane and asked her, "Should we invite those guys over? We have some extra hamburgers." She thought it was a good idea, so they invited the men over and shared both food and fellowship. Being a large and strong man who had worked for years as a logger, Rocky is not easily intimidated, so the appearance of the homeless men did not frighten him. Instead, he took the opportunity to boldly share the love of Christ with them.

The next week at church, Rocky was so excited about what happened in the park that he shared it with me after the service.

Unable to contain his zeal, he invited some of his friends and their families to go back to the park and share in this experience. Although our church had no programmed ministry to the homeless, Rocky, Diane, and these other families began to develop one simply out of their passion as disciples.

After feeding a dozen people the second week, Rocky approached me after the service on week three. He was strapped for cash. "Tri, this is a great thing in the park and we're doing what you told us to do from the pulpit, but I can't afford this any more," he told me. When I asked him what he needed, he replied, "I just need a little money to buy some hamburgers." After giving him $20, I watched him head for the park. Though I was still curious about what might emerge, I wanted to underwrite him personally for at least one more week.

The following Sunday Rocky returned excited as ever. I realized that this was one of those snowballs rolling downhill – a snowball that I didn't want to break up. After that week, I went to our finance team and suggested that we underwrite Rocky and give him a small budget so he could keep feeding the homeless and get more people involved. At this point, I had said nothing from the pulpit about what was happening. I was just watching it emerge out of the culture of the church.

This homeless ministry began to grow until Rocky needed more than just hamburger meat; he needed more grills and a trailer to take them to the park. Our church began to provide for Rocky's homeless ministry because we saw it as a legitimate discipling ministry, which fit the vision of the church. What started with an innocent invitation to some homeless men in a park has grown to a thriving ministry at the time of this writing called, "Feeding God's Children." This ministry feeds 200-300 people every Sunday after church in the same park where it all started. We have expanded this ministry with a partnership with the local men and women's rescue missions, helping bus their people to church for Sunday services. The ministry also includes ranchers in the Owyhee Mountains who provide us with cattle. We have a team who transport the cattle to a local butcher who donates his time as well. Because this ministry has grown to such a degree, we had to build a walk-in freezer in our benevolence center to hold all the donated food needed to make it happen each week. We just kept the snowball rolling.

CULTIVATING A CULTURE

In some ways, shaping a culture is easier than starting one from scratch, but this is only true if the culture you have is a healthy one. An unhealthy culture is difficult to reverse and must be handled with care and patience.

The old adage "one bad apple can spoil the whole bunch" is

true when it comes to the delicate culture of church life. Most pastors and leaders have experienced this on some level. We have seen entire home groups lost because of a wounded leader, and we have seen ministries damaged by disgruntled people. Often this is because people tend to enter into our church cultures with old baggage, preconceived ideas about church life, and agendas that are contrary to the vision and values of our church. Sooner or later they will expose their disappointments, generally in harmful ways. They might call the church "non-relational" when the truth is they did not get the personal attention from the church leader-

> When the culture is disrupted or damaged, it will almost always disrupt momentum.

ship they had expected. Smaller churches are especially vulnerable to the "bad apple" syndrome, and if the leadership is not skilled at tactful and loving confrontation, the "whole bunch" can be poisoned beyond repair. This is often the first sign of a potential church split. When the culture is disrupted or damaged, it will almost always disrupt momentum. For this reason I continually remind pastors to be proactive when it comes to culture.

There are three antidotes that can stop this poison from spreading in a church. The first is *a clear statement of vision and values.* This ensures that you will not be swayed by wrong agendas.

71

The second is to *develop healthy confrontational skills*. Oftentimes I have observed pastors who let unhealthy cultures fester far too long. When they finally get around to bringing correction, they come off much too strong. I encourage my leaders to never get too worked up over things. I tell them to take care of business as problems arise, and always remember that we are the ones who asked God to send us lost and broken people in the first place.

The third antidote is to *be above reproach in all that you do*. You must have the delicate balance of never being too controlling, yet possessing the confidence in yourself to lead with strength. Be gentile and loving, but unchanging in your convictions.

> Good attitudes are contagious; somehow they communicate hope and victory.

While overseeing over a hundred churches, I had a unique vantage point to see many types of church cultures. I recognized the impact attitudes make on the welfare of the community culture. One of the most damaging elements that can be introduced to a ministry's culture is negativity or bad attitudes.

At some point everyone has experienced the impact of good and bad attitudes. We all know when someone walks in a room with a positive attitude he or she has a way of bringing sunshine. Good attitudes are contagious; somehow they communicate hope and victory. A good attitude will inspire people to keep going even in the worst of times. A good attitude will communicate the belief that "in Christ all things are possible." On the other hand, a bad attitude has a tendency to bring defeat and gloom. Remember the Winnie the Pooh character, Eeyore? He was the great pessimist who always seemed to view life from the negative side. People with the Eeyore syndrome have a tendency to suck the life out of a healthy church culture. While they call themselves "realists," they constantly tell the group why things are wrong, always seeing the bad in both people and situations. The ultimate reason that bad attitudes are death to vision is because they reinforce the idea that impossible dreams are impossible to achieve. Bad attitudes quench faith.

The Apostle Paul told the Ephesians that one of the characteristics of the new life in Christ was a transformed attitude:

But that isn't what you were taught when you learned about Christ. Since you have heard all about him and have learned the truth that is in Jesus, throw off your old evil nature and your former way of life, which is rotten through and through, full of lust and deception. Instead, there must be a spiritual renewal of your thoughts and attitudes. You must display a new nature because you are a new person, created in God's likeness – righteous, holy, and true.

– EPHESIANS 4: 20-24

I believe Paul said this because he too had firsthand experience with church life. He knew one characteristic of the "old man" is a defeating attitude that would kill a healthy church culture. As a result, he gave counsel as to how we might obtain victory over unsanctified attitudes. In the following eight verses (Ephesians 4: 25-32), Paul gave seven pointers on how we must live so that our negative attitudes would not persist and destroy what God was doing within our community.

Through the years I have encouraged leaders to reinforce these principles over and over; I especially stress them with my leadership team. For this reason, I faithfully dedicate one session of our leadership development class to teaching this passage in Ephesians and reinforcing the value of sanctified attitudes.

For the rest of this chapter, we will look at how we built a culture of discipleship at our church and how you can use some of these same principles and apply them to the shaping of the culture within your own church.

Paul's Counsel for Sanctified Attitudes

1. Good attitudes begin with honesty. Not only do we need to admit when our attitudes are going sour, but we need to be around people who are willing to call us on those bad attitudes. (vs. 25: "So put away all falsehood and 'tell your neighbor the truth' because we belong to each other.")

2. Don't let your bad attitude have time to brew. Deal with it before it has time to do real damage. Unresolved conflict will kill your culture. It is especially the responsibility of leadership to go after attitudes that are damaging the community. (vs. 26: "And 'don't sin by letting anger gain control over you.' Don't let the sun go down while you are still angry.")

3. Know that if the devil can damage your culture, he can take down the church. We must be spiritually mature when it comes to attitudes. Remember, the devil is a liar and a deceiver. He will make you want to think the worst. (vs. 27: "for anger gives a mighty foothold to the devil.")

4. When you feel like doing something negative because of your attitude, do the opposite. Don't destroy the culture; add to it. (vs. 28: "If you are a thief, stop stealing. Begin using your hands for honest work, and then give generously to others in need.")

5. Gossip and negative talk are unwholesome. Remember, a bad attitude will always manifest itself through the words of our mouths. Leaders especially must discipline themselves to only speak words that will edify and build up the community. (vs. 29: "Don't use foul or abusive language. Let everything you say be good and helpful, so that your words will be an encouragement to those who hear them.")

6. It is important for any Christian to remember the Holy Spirit is listening and cares about our attitudes. Our bad attitudes actually grieve God.

(vs. 30: " And do not bring sorrow to God's Holy Spirit by the way you live. Remember, he is the one who has identified you as his own, guaranteeing that you will be saved on the day of redemption.")

7. And finally, remember that bad attitudes are generally rooted in woundedness. I always say, "The only way someone can get your goat is if you have a goat to get; and Jesus came to take care of the goat." In other words, our bad attitudes generally manifest when something or someone has pushed our button that is rooted in unresolved sin issues. To rid ourselves of poisoned attitudes, we must receive the full provision of the cross. We must be healed by Jesus of the bitterness and anger that would destroy our lives and relationships. (vs. 31-32: "Get rid of all bitterness, rage, anger, harsh words, and slander, as well as all types of malicious behavior. Instead, be kind to each other, tenderhearted, forgiving one another, just as God through Christ has forgiven you.")

A Culture of Love

As our church began to grow, many exciting things began to emerge out of the church culture, such as the homeless ministry. But I also began to notice that our culture was not entirely healthy. (While had bumper stickers that stated, "Come as you are! You'll be loved!" But, somehow, it didn't always seem like we were reaching out in love to each other as well as newcomers. So, I challenged our people to remove those stickers until they actually lived those words.) I began to feel ineffective as a leader, which emerged out of what I saw as a deficit in our ability to fulfill our God-given vision. That vision for us is developing authentic followers of Christ. The burning question in my heart was this: "Are people's lives really being transformed?" I wasn't sure that I was seeing the fruit of this and it disturbed me.

If you want to build a community of love, you really have to be a community of trust. People who truly love each other are people who trust each other, who are faithful, who understand the vision and purpose, working together with one heart and one mind.

One of the things I've observed in churches is that so many of them experience leadership explosions. Every time there is a blow up or hiccup in the leadership team, it sets the church back, sometimes a year or two. The church never has the opportunity to build momentum and move into a place of great productivity and fruitfulness. From the very beginning of our church, I recognized the need to build leaders from the ground up, to "home grow" our people so that they not only trusted and understood me, but also trusted and understood my passion for building a church that disciples people into Christian maturity.

Early in our church planting adventure, I discovered another mistake many pastors make. In their rush to assemble a leadership team, they select elders too early. One Christian leader suggested to me in the beginning stages of our church that I wait to appoint elders in our church for at least seven years. He said I would not even know who was going to stick around until I gave the church some time to develop. I took that advice and began building *counsels*, but not *eldership* boards. There was accountability, but in the first phases they were transitory leaders.

As I looked to the Bible for a model that would work in building our church, I found it in Luke 6. Up to that point in Jesus' ministry, He had been doing the entire ministry Himself. He had done all the teaching, performed all the healings and miracles. He had yet to select His 12 disciples. But He was preparing His followers for what was next, and this particular passage deals with the day that Jesus finally selected them.

One day soon afterward Jesus went to a mountain to pray, and he prayed to God all night. At daybreak he called together all of his dis-

ciples and chose twelve of them to be apostles.

– LUKE 6:12-13

After Jesus identified and named the 12 disciples, the story continues.

When they came down the slopes of the mountain, the disciples stood with Jesus on a large, level area, surrounded by many of his follow-ers and by the crowds. There were people from all over Judea and from Jerusalem and from as far north as the seacoasts of Tyre and Sidon. They had come to hear him and to be healed, and Jesus cast out many evil spirits. Everyone was trying to touch him, because healing power went out from him, and they were all cured.

— LUKE 6:17-19

Two facets surrounding this passage jumped out at me. First, I noticed there were four reasons people gathered around Jesus. They came because they wanted to **be taught and learn truth**. They came because they wanted to **be healed** from whatever it was that was afflicting them – emotional, physical or spiritual "dis-eases." They came to **be set free from the bondage in their lives**. They came because they wanted to **be close and touch Him** because power was coming from Him. Essentially, these are the four reasons anybody comes to church. They come to be taught, to be healed, to be set free, and to be close to the Lord.

The second thing I noticed was that there were three designations of groups of people. First, there were the *throngs* (or multitudes or crowds). There was the mass of people who were coming from all over to see Jesus. But of that mass, there was another group that was designated as the *multitude of disciples*, possibly the 70 or the 120 that is talked about later in the Gospels. I see a difference in these people when compared to the throngs. These people had already committed to following Jesus. They did not show up just for this event; they traveled with Him, following Him from town to town. It was out of the multitudes of disciples that Jesus chose 12 and named them *disciples*. And we know of those twelve, there were three – Peter, James, and John – who spent extra time with Jesus. They were with Him at the transfiguration. They were with him on a hillside over Jerusalem when He was talking about the last days. They were the ones He sent ahead to prepare for the Passover. They ultimately became the high profile leaders of the church of Jerusalem in its early stages.

Each person from all three of these groups came for the same reasons at one point in their journey. However, there had to be a transition between a throng mentality and a multitude of disciples' mentality. And there was also a transition between the multitudes of disciples to one of the 12 disciples. My heart has always been to make disciples – authentic, mature, spirit-filled, reproducible Christians. So, I asked myself, what is the difference in these groups?

I realized that the throngs are *consumers*. They come to get. They come because they have needs and they want to get those needs met. They come because they want to be healed, they want to be delivered, they want to be close to God. They want for themselves and they have great needs. All of us who are authentic Christians were members of the throngs at one point. We all had needs to be met, because until we received, we really had nothing to give. It can cause a church a lot of strife when empty people are trying to give what they do not possess. I wanted to set up a system by which I could help people develop into mature Christians. When people truly experience the love of God and therefore have that love to give, then a true community of love, care, and outreach can exist. I knew I *couldn't* do it by myself – and Jesus *didn't* do it by Himself either. He trained and deployed this group of people to carry out the work of the Kingdom.

As a result of these principles from Luke 6, I believed the Lord gave me a process and a plan to usher people from the throng mentality into discipleship.

The multitudes of disciples were the ones who made the shift from a throng mentality to a discipleship mentality, which was this: "I want to be taught so I can teach. I want to be healed so I could be an instrument to heal others. I want to be set free so I might lend a hand to help others be set free from their bondage and addiction. I want to be close to the Lord so I can usher others into the Lord's presence. I want to get in order to give, not just get to get." This is how I define someone who has made this transition. I also recognized that in order to have a multitude of disciples, you have to have people in place who have already made the choice to disciple others.

In my mind, the 12 disciples are these people who are discipling. In the case of the local church, this is the lay leadership of the church, people leading the small groups, the nursery, the men's ministry, etc. They are people who are stepping into this second arena and saying, "I get to give." Out of this group of disciplers there are some that begin to emerge as the "three." The people who fit into this category become the eldership, or leaders of leaders, of the church.

In processing this information, we developed a system at Vineyard Boise where people could progress from crowd mentality into discipleship. It also provided opportunity for the Lord to reveal to us those who were leading so we could pull them into the leadership arena. I had no interest in guessing who my elders might be by measuring whether they were charismatic people, or had a good business background, or seemed to understand organization. John Wimber always said, "You know your elders because they eld," meaning you know who your elders are because they are doing the work of the ministry more than the others.

The Culture Component

Developing a Culture of Leadership

T o foster a culture within our church that engaged people at these different stages in their discipleship, we implemented a new structure. Remember, this is merely a tool we used to build a culture of healthy leadership while pursuing our God-given vision of developing authentic disciples. As we talk about what we have done at Vineyard Boise, keep in mind the vision for your ministry and how these principles could apply. On the following page is a diagram of our system. While drawing it for my friend Ed McGlasson one day he dubbed it the "Power Flower," and the name has since stuck.

Look at the diagram on the following page, then we will begin to break down each section of the "Power Flower."

CULTURE   Power Flower Culture Circles

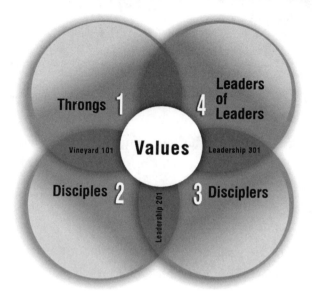

It is important to understand that the center of everything you do is based on the values you establish among those you are leading. People will perceive these values more from what they see you do than by those things you say. Ultimately, communicating those values in a way that changes people's lives is what a leader is trying to achieve. The fruit of your values is what you want to see emerging in the hearts and lives of your people.

The Center Circle: Core Values

The center of the Power Flower consists of the core values of our church:

1. Worshiping God, in the freedom of the Spirit

2. Clear, accurate, biblical teaching, which produces sound doctrine

3. Prayer and Intercession

4. Ministry
   · Ministering with the gifts of the Spirit in operation
   · Benevolence and ministry to the poor, widows, orphans, and hurting
   · Ministering the love of Jesus to the sick and hurting by praying for healing and looking for God to provide signs and wonders

5. Reproduction
   · Equipping the saints for the work of the ministry and the raising up of mature Christian disciples and leaders.
   · Evangelistic outreach — reaching the unsaved and unchurched in our community with the Gospel
   · Commitment to missions — church planting at home, world missions abroad

6. Fellowship
   · Building relationships together within the local church body
   · Unity within the whole Body of Christ — relationship with other local churches

7. Stewardship
   · Giving time, money, and resources to the Kingdom
   · Preserving God's gift of creation

As we move through this model, it is important to remember that all values must start from the top of the organization and filter down to the people whose lives you are trying to influence. I will give you an example. During the disillusionment period I experienced in 1995, one of the things that bothered me was our church's lack of zeal for worship. In the Vineyard we have always stated that worshipping God is our highest value. To my disappointment, I observed that our people had lost the hunger to worship during the Sunday morning services. As is characteristic of most pastors, I decided to preach a series of messages on the subject in hopes of revitalizing this very critical value in the church. Although it seemed to help for a while, my efforts proved short lived.

One morning during worship I noticed that my elders and many key leaders were in the back of the room, unengaged during the worship time. It appeared to me that they had entered a "worker mentality" during the service rather than engaging in the very thing that brought them into the ministry in the first place. During our next elders meeting I addressed the issue, not in a confronting way, but as their pastor. I encouraged them to work one service and fully engage with the Lord for their own benefit at the other. (This is one reason I feel so strongly about churches having at least two services. Even if the size of a church could get by without it, a church's workforce must receive if they have any hope of being able to give.) I will never forget how my elders responded that day. If you ask me, it was a pivotal moment in the life of Vineyard Boise. After a moment of silence, I began to see tears flowing down several of their cheeks; then outward weeping broke out. A spirit of repentance hit the room followed by spontaneous prayer asking God to birth in us again a heart for worship.

This rekindled passion for worship began to filter down to our leaders as they saw our elders worship. And from them, it passed into our weekly small groups. Eventually, heart-felt worship returned to our Sunday morning worship service.

> Values must move from the top down.

Values must move from the top down. If you want your church to be a praying church, then you must have leaders who value and practice a life of prayer. If you want the value of servanthood and compassion to permeate your fellowship then you must have leaders who are servants and demonstrate love in action. This is one reason that I am so committed to our process of discipleship. As we stay consistent in this process, we end up with leaders who have demonstrated the practice of these core values before they ever are allowed to enter into a leadership role. In my mind, this is crucial for any church that desires to bring people to a place of authentic and mature Christianity.

THE FIRST CIRCLE: THE CROWD

In examining the first circle (see diagram on the opposite page), we find that it largely starts with evangelism. People are drawn into the life of the church, usually by the invitation from someone they know. Primarily, people enter into our corporate life during the weekend services or special events. They experience life in a large group – corporate worship, corporate teaching, corporate ministry. However, for the momentum in their lives to continue, the involvement must not stop there. They must be provided with an invitation to further connect within the life of the church – this could be a small group, Bible study, or accountability group. People may not respond immediately, but our culture in the first circle is one of inclusion and encouragement towards participation.

Determining if someone is in the first circle is simple. For our church, it goes back to our credo, "Come as you are – you'll be loved!" The rule of engagement is simple; people can enter into fellowship at Vineyard Boise with no strings attached. However, we do not want to see people remain in this circle forever. We have a specific strategy on how to move them from being part of the crowd toward a life of engaged discipleship.

One of the goals of the leadership team that oversees the first circle is to host "Vineyard 101" classes at least four times a year. This class is the gateway to Circle 2, the discipleship circle. The

CULTURE   Power Flower Culture Circles

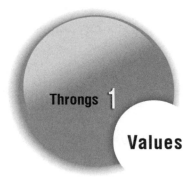

Throngs 1

Values

101 class is the best place we have found to explain discipleship to the people and how they can take more advantage of the life inside Vineyard Boise. Our class is currently structured to run one night a week for four weeks. During this time we hope to establish a pattern in the participants of giving one night a week to pursuing a life of discipleship.

During Vineyard 101 we worship, provide a history of the Vineyard movement and Vineyard Boise, share with them how we desire to see God work in their lives, and explain to them what our expectations are of them should they make a commitment to the church. In some churches this could serve as a membership class (although our church has no formal membership at this time).

It is also during this class that we introduce people to small group dynamics. The first half of each meeting is lecture based, but the second half is broken down into small groups no larger than 10 people. Many of our church's small group leaders return to the 101 class to help lead these groups and much of our success has been due to their continued involvement.

The first night, after the groups have been formed, our small group leaders ask simple, non-threatening questions like, "Who are you?" and "How did you happen to come to the Vineyard?" Just those two questions reveal a lot about people. The second night the questions go a little bit deeper. The leaders ask, "What do you hope the Lord would do with your life?" And the third night after our church's vision and values have been discussed, our leaders ask, "What do you want to do for the Lord?" and "How can I help you get there?" Our final night of the course is exciting. Some people give their lives to Christ and others take the opportunity to get baptized. This last night our small group leaders invite them to come to their own home group the following week. They already know their leader and have been establishing trust with them, which helps launch them into the small group life and discipleship.

The Lure of Authenticity

When Tempe McFarlane first walked through the doors of Vineyard Boise, her life was in shambles. Her marriage was quickly crumbling, her job was losing its satisfaction, and emptiness had found a home in her heart. Upon her sister's encouragement, Tempe decided to visit the Vineyard.

"When I walked into the church, there were tables and chairs throughout the sanctuary," Tempe recalls. "It was like we had to make friends when we came to church. And I loved that! People served me coffee – it instantly felt like home."

"At the time, I was going to work everyday in a business suit, so it was very relaxing to go to church without having to dress up. I looked around the church and saw that people were in their Levi's. It was then that I started to realize how true the church's slogan of 'come as you are' really was."

On one of Tempe's early visits to Vineyard Boise, someone pointed out a poster to her.

> Wanted: Drug addicts, the lonely, the beat up
> Purpose: To be cleansed and made holy
> Come as you are!

"When I saw the poster, I thought, 'Are these types of people really welcome here?' But I knew the answer was, 'yes.' I was coming from a legalistic, 'do-this-do-that' mentality, but I began to realize how much God loved me, and how He wanted me to be real. I was drawn to that. I was drawn to these people who were authentic."

Tempe made a friend named Carrie and continued to visit the church. "Carrie was friendly and we soon became friends," Tempe said. "It seemed like a lot of places I went, everyone had their certain cliques, but not at the Vineyard. Her friendship was one of the things that drew me, but it was much more than that. The way people loved me there and served me there. The hosts and the greeters were so kind — they even refilled my coffee!

"I came to church with expectations that people in church were perfect. I wasn't sure if I was going to fit in with them. But as I began building relationships with them, I realized that I could just be myself. And then I heard Pastor Tri speak. He twisted a few words around in the delivery of his sermon and I thought, 'This is so cool. This guy is not perfect!' Here was somebody who was absolutely authentic. He was speaking about love and loving each other. He blew away my concept of unapproachable and perfect preachers. It's funny how the little things make a big difference."

These days Tempe is interested in seeing other people experience the same life-changing power of Christ that restored her marriage and rooted out the emptiness in her heart. On Sunday mornings, you'll find her meeting new people who walk through the doors of Vineyard Boise. As the Director of Community Outreach, Tempe is doing what she does best.

"My heart is that when people walk through the doors of our church, someone is connecting with them with a 'hello' and a friendly smile so they feel like they are significant and loved right away," Tempe said. "This is a friendly place. It is very contagious!"

Upon entering the church, it's evident that there is a vibrant culture among those who have a heart to connect seekers and newcomers into the church. You can see it immediately from the greeters who freely give both directions and hugs.

"The culture is everything," Tempe said. "We have people in their 40's who have never been to church, people raised in a different religion, from different church settings, and people who are church shopping. So, there is an instant need for us to connect with them, wherever they are, by being authentic and genuine, as well as helpful. We want them to feel like they belong."

SEEKER-SENSITIVE AND AUTHENTIC DISCIPLESHIP?

In examining this first circle, it is important to maintain a balance between being a seeker-sensitive church and being a church that makes genuine disciples. While some people believe the two cannot co-exist, I believe they not only can exist, but they must exist together.

Once I visited a church that is known for its seeker-sensitive approach to ministry. But instead of talking to the church leadership, whom I knew was sold on the methodology of being seeker-friendly, I casually started conversations with anyone who would openly talk to me. Maybe it was the luck of the draw, but one of the first people I bumped into was an usher who had been serving in his role for almost three years. In the context of the conversation, I learned that he had never made a commitment to follow the Lord. A closer look at the church showed me that most of the effort of the church was focused on the Sunday morning event; and it truly was an event. It was a wonderful time. The production of the morning was flawless, the music professional, the teaching inspirational and the use of video and PowerPoint was even impressive to someone like me who is technologically inept. But another thing I noticed was the mid-week small groups and Bible studies were out of proportion to the number of people who showed up on Sunday. I am not being critical because I am the first to know that different pastors have different passions and methods of implementing their vision. However, it challenged me to look at what we were doing in Boise.

A positive observation I made of the seeker-sensitive church was that it was certainly attracting more people than we were. As a result, they had a much bigger fishing pond from which to catch people for the purpose of moving them from the crowd into discipleship arenas. My conclusion was that there needed to be balance between building a large crowd and building a church that is passionate about discipleship. I realized that Sunday needed to be, on some levels, attractive to the unchurched. The unchurched have consumer mentalities, and rightfully so. All of us initially came to church because we had needs that we were driven to have met. For most people, Sunday is a time to receive. If we frighten the unsaved away on their first visit, we will never have the privilege of discipling them later. I tell our people that Sunday has to be safe for people who have little or no grid for church life. In that sense, it must be "seeker-sensitive." Although we never want to deny the Holy Spirit to have freedom among us, we must follow Paul's counsel in 1 Corinthians 14 and be careful not to overwhelm our guests with charismatic activity.

Though we clearly and unashamedly preach the truth about Jesus without any reservation, we offer most of our Spirit-led ministry on Sunday mornings at the end of the services. This allows people the freedom to leave the sanctuary to pursue fellowship with those who invited them to church, while providing the opportunity for those who need ministry and prayer to receive it.

Most of the ministry that exemplifies the charisma takes place in our second circle, the arena of discipleship and community life. In this way, the church has continually grown numerically through the culture we have created in Circle 1, without sacrificing the values we pursue whole-heartedly in our life of discipleship together.

THE SECOND CIRCLE: MULTITUDES OF DISCIPLES

Once a person has an understanding of the vision of Vineyard Boise – making mature, reproducible, Spirit-filled, Christian disciples – and has committed to participating in that life with us (usually as a result of our Vineyard 101 class), he moves from the crowd mentality into discipleship (see diagram on next page). We watch as they begin to give of their life, time, and resources for serving others. Their commitment to the Lord strengthens as they see what it means to lay one's life down. Instead of just coming to church on Sundays to receive, they begin to receive so they can give. Those who are serious about their faith begin to emerge.

By weaving this value of raising up authentic disciples into the culture of our church leadership, our small group leaders begin to look for people in the second circle who are bearing fruit through

Power Flower Culture Circles

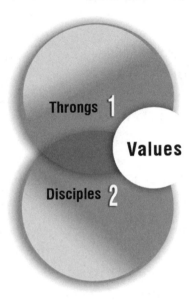

their commitment to God, their fellowship with other believers, and their service to the world. Our small group leaders are encouraged and trained to be on the lookout for potential leaders. They consider those in their group who could take their place or lead another group. As they see these people emerge, the leader invites them to our "Leadership 201" class, a multiple-week leadership development course which prepares emerging leaders for the responsibility in the third circle.

Making Disciples

When Mike Freeman began attending Vineyard Boise, the last thing he wanted to do was get involved in leadership. After leading a local church through a long storm as the senior pastor, Mike and his wife LaWayne laid down the pastorate and were simply looking for a place to reconnect with other believers when they walked through the doors of the Vineyard.

"Working 40 hours a week in a secular job was fine for me," Mike said, "I had no expectations of going anywhere and moving up the ministry ladder when I started coming to Vineyard Boise. LaWayne and I were just basking in our experience here. We weren't in a real hurry to do anything."

But even when the Freemans began to get actively involved in the church, they received no special passes because of their pastoral background. Like everyone else in the church, they entered at Circle 1.

"We went through the 101 class, and then we kept going back again and again to lead others through it," said Mike, now an associate pastor on staff at Vineyard Boise. "We never got tired of hearing the stories and vision of the church."

Eventually, Mike and LaWayne were asked to help lead in the small group they were a part of, and then oversee other groups as well. They began serving throughout the church, receiving ministry and healing in their own lives, while at the same time giving life out to many others.

"We weren't looking for position," Mike said. "I didn't fathom that I could step into leadership here because I was busy relearning a Christian walk with the new shoes of the Kingdom of God and grace. I had been teaching Bible class for a couple of decades, but I hadn't really learned what it meant to be ministering the Gospel to people."

In his current role as overseer of adult education and small group ministry, Mike's main emphasis is on helping raise up disciples, not getting people from one circle to the next. Discipleship is the vision of the church, not making everyone leaders.

"We want to get people plugged into relationships in the church because that's where discipleship begins to take shape," Mike said. "In our

101 class, we are able to sell people on the vision of what we're doing, of how we want to help them grow and mature in their relationship with God as they connect with others. We show them how they can move from being a spectator to being a participant."

While the size of the church and amount of people could feel overwhelming, Mike explains how the church can feel much smaller once someone has connected.

"What I tell them is that the bigger the church is, the smaller it has to be," Mike said. "One of the most natural ways to do this is to participate in a ministry alongside other people. Then as you develop relationships with those you are working with, you will recognize their faces and connect with them when you see them again in church. This will transform your Sunday morning experience. It begins the process of fellowship and you start to feel you belong. It begins to snowball, and your transformation into discipleship takes on a richness that you wouldn't have imagined the first time you came to church and sat looking at the back of everyone's head."

Ultimately, the circles help identify an experience for those interested in getting involved or those who are just beginning to plug into the church.

"In our 101 class, if someone says, 'I'd like to go help the poor,' then we can show them how they can do that," Mike said. "Some people plug in there and they never leave. People aren't trying to move and work the circles as much as it is a natural progression in people's lives. What we desire most is to see people get discipled."

By weaving this value of raising up authentic disciples into the culture of our church leadership, our small group leaders begin to look for people in the second circle who are bearing fruit through their commitment to God, their fellowship with other believers, and their service to the world. Our small group leaders are encouraged and trained to be on the lookout for potential leaders. They consider those in their group who could take their place or lead another group. As they see these people emerge, the leader invites them to our "Leadership 201" class, a multiple-week leadership development course which prepares emerging leaders for the responsibility in the third circle.

In this course, we teach leadership principles which represent our values. We talk about our leaders' attitudes, the "Power Flower," our management system, and how to resolve conflict so we can keep our culture healthy and vibrant. We also talk about mature leadership and mature Christianity. Again, we reaffirm our goal of building disciples who are mature and authentic in their relationship with Christ and others.

Completing Leadership 201 does not make a person a leader. The purpose of the class is to expose our principles of leadership to these emerging leaders, but it is up to our current leaders to launch these people into roles and responsibilities when they are ready. This helps us release leaders based on relationship and accountability, not merely picking a person because of their previous experience, zeal or stature. All of these may be good qualities, but we are looking for God's timing for these future leaders.

THE THIRD CIRCLE: THE TWELVE

Once a leader has been released into ministry they are closely monitored and nurtured by other leaders. One thing we look for are those who not only are good at running their area of ministry, but those who have a knack for reproducing leaders themselves. Once a leader shows a pattern of releasing others into ministry, we recognize this person may not simply be a leader, but a leader of leaders. In my mind, this is one of the important elements of eldership. An elder is someone who understands how to develop ministry and maintain ministry. When we see someone who can nurture and monitor many leaders and not just have a ministry unto themselves, we invite that person into the fourth circle, which begins with our "Leadership 301" retreat (see diagram on opposite page).

Our Leadership 301 retreat is an annual meeting for the leaders of leaders of Vineyard Boise. At this time, I share my heart for the church with them. We strategically evaluate the church, looking at what the Lord has done in our church over the past year. We also examine the three points in the synergy triangle: Do the people understand the vision? Is our culture healthy and thriving?

Is our structure serving the culture, or are our people becoming frustrated because of a lack of structure or too much structure? We also ask hard questions, such as "Do we have programs that we don't really need any more?" Sometimes, this can be uncomfortable, but we must take a long look at the church and review our goals and objectives for the next year. It's a time of reflection but also of dreaming and looking into the future.

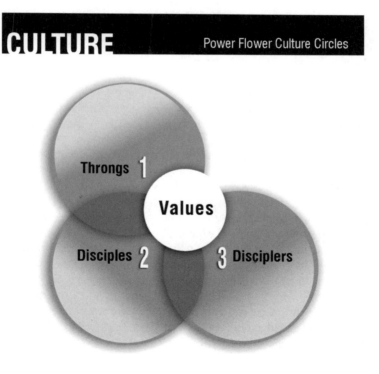

CULTURE Power Flower Culture Circles

Throngs 1

Values

Disciples 2   3 Disciplers

Giving Away Leadership

When Chad Estes began attending Vineyard Boise, his experience with church leaders had been marked with broken trust. And it was a simple, yet courageous, comment by the senior pastor from the platform that caught the attention of Chad and his wife Jamie.

"During the announcements the week before, some guys had been goofing around on stage and offended some people," Chad recalled. "But instead of blaming them, Tri stood up in front of the church the following week and took responsibility, saying that the buck stopped with him. I was so impressed that this leader was secure enough to take this criticism and not pass it off on others. That is when my wife Jamie and I started thinking that this church could be our home."

And while it was Tri's unwillingness to pass off blame that captured Chad and Jamie's attention, it was Tri's willingness to give away leadership that lured them back into ministry. Serving as a technical writer for a major computer innovator, Chad was asked to help write "The Matrix Manual" (see Section IV) along with Tri. Through developing relationships with Vineyard Boise's leaders while writing the manual, he saw the formula for successful church leadership.

"One of the reasons our church has grown so quickly and so steadily is that Tri has been willing to give leadership away," Chad said. "I have pastors of both large and small churches call me every week looking for our secrets for church growth. What I tell them is that I have found a leader who is secure enough in his calling that he isn't afraid to work with other people."

"As a result, a culture has been developed where people know that they can play. They know it is okay for them to lead and to take responsibility and help this church grow. Because of the way we're structured, there are more leadership opportunities. Once somebody begins to lead, they really begin to own it and take responsibility for it. Our church has transitioned from the place where Tri was responsible for everything as the

pioneer to where he is not usually responsible for any specific min
the church."

Using the synergy model, Vineyard Boise has revamped the way ministry leaders report and how each ministry is monitored because of the
sheer size of the church. However, the consistent value of giving away
leadership has helped create a healthy culture within the Circle 3 leaders.

"Often leaders get nervous and feel threatened when those around
them begin succeeding," Chad said. "But If you really have a vision for
your church to grow and you give others opportunities, your church will
benefit from it. Because he has given leadership opportunities away, our
leaders are really loyal to Tri. He has created a culture of trust that makes
you want to participate.

"And as we have learned first-hand the importance of passing values
from the top down, our leaders have learned how to give away ministry as
well. That value has been clearly demonstrated many times by Tri, and we
have all integrated that value into the way we do ministry as well."

Tri has also been fearless when it came time to make necessary
changes, according to Chad.

"We've changed our structure here many times over the years to
make it fit us," Chad said. "I've seen other churches set in their ways of
how they function together. It has limited their church and kept them from
getting where they desire to go. Tri has never been afraid to make those
changes. It's also exciting for us as a staff. When you trust and believe that
your leader wants you to succeed, you're more likely to risk making
changes in order to be successful with what God has put in your heart to
do."

THE FOURTH CIRCLE: THE THREE

One of the results of our 301 retreat is that we see the leaders of leaders step forward into Circle 4 (see diagram on opposite page). Some of these leaders have pastoral roles, some of them are directors and overseers, some of them are the elders for Vineyard Boise.

Our Circle 4 leaders' primary job is to care for their Circle 3 leaders, who disciple the second circle, who reach back into the first circle and encourage them towards discipleship. The lion's share of my job as the senior pastor is to care for our Circle 4 leaders. They have budgets and have to turn in yearly objectives and goals. They have to be monitored and, more than anything, cared for and pastored. They have to be healthy. If these people go south, they can get the church in trouble. So, I keep a pulse on their spiritual life and their ministries. I develop closer relationships with these people than anyone else in the church. At times, I sit down with them and help them problem-solve or create. I listen to their ideas and dreams and help them achieve what God has placed on their heart. Also, it is my role to see how I can underwrite and raise

> The lion's share of my job as the senior pastor is to care for our Circle 4 leaders.

money to see those ministries happen.

It is out of this level of leadership that we want to see our church planters and missionaries emerge. Then we know we are sending out our best, those who have proven themselves in serving, in leading, in reproducing themselves and reproducing ministries.

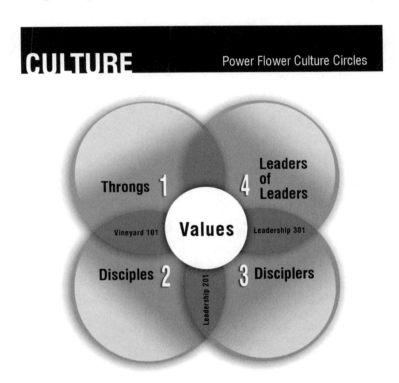

CULTURE   Power Flower Culture Circles

Throngs 1

4 Leaders of Leaders

Vineyard 101   Values   Leadership 301

Disciples 2   Leadership 201   3 Disciplers

From the Pew to the Pastorate

Working as a finish carpenter, Ken Myers often contemplated entering the ministry as a pastor. And after a few years of naturally moving through the leadership circles at Vineyard Boise, he finally made a familiar transition from carpenter to pastor.

"I always thought I was called to be a pastor, but I wanted to wait and learn and see God actually doing it on His own without me forcing it," Myers said. "It was waiting to let the Lord go before me. You can desire all you want, but you don't want to be premature and get ahead of God."

While the desire to become a pastor was within Ken's heart, it took getting the opportunity to exercise his pastoral gifting in a safe environment before the desire reached a boiling point. And while he had a desire to church plant, he began to faithfully serve in different areas of the church and continued to grow.

"I came into the first circle and saw that God had more for me," Myers said. "I wanted to get involved in the community life of the church and be part of the body of Christ rather than just an observer. As I began building relationships, I began to see there are so many people out there who need to be discipled."

Ken and his wife Rachel's ability to disciple others within their small group was recognized by his small group leader. Not long after that, the Myers were leading their own small group, and before long, they had planted a handful of small groups out of their own. Ken and Rachel's passion to lead and serve others resulted in an invitation to lead the church's prayer ministry.

"At that point, God began to define my vision, which was similar to what was occurring at Vineyard Boise but different," said Ken. "So, I told Tri that I wanted to plant a church. Rachel and I moved to Caldwell, Idaho, where we are doing the same thing."

The "same thing" Myers refers to is that of recognizing the talents and gifts of those serving God around him and releasing them in ministry as well.

As someone who simply entered the church doors looking to grow closer to Christ, Myers left with some valuable life-changing principles and a solid understanding of what it takes to lead others in ministry.

"I'm still using the same method of leadership reproduction for our church," Myers said. "I believe God sends you people that have the gifts you don't – and you have to empower them and free them up to do what they were created to do – that is one of the keys to the leadership development I have learned from Tri."

Within Circle 4 there are various groups of leaders. First of all, there are the elders. In my case, I have seven elders. I think that's a good-sized and manageable group. They are the spiritual oversight for our church. They are actually "elding" other Circle 4 leaders for me because, as the group has grown, I've needed help in overseeing all of our ministries and caring for our leaders. Each elder has a board of their own, which we call "macro teams," groups which help them brainstorm and give wisdom and insight for decision making.

For example, our children's ministry has its own macro team. Our elementary school has a board of education. Our benevolence ministry has a benevolence board to determine how the money for the poor should be spent each week. These teams also help their leaders build infrastructure and develop vision for their ministries.

Some of our Circle 4 leaders are pastors (we have both lay pastors as well as staff pastors) and some are ministry directors.

Every Circle 4 leader attends a weekly prayer meeting and a weekly staff meeting. These leaders develop objectives, goals, and budgets on a yearly basis. They are held in high accountability, whether they are on staff or lay leaders. To the degree that these people succeed is the degree to which our church grows and bears fruit. My role as a senior pastor is to serve these people, helping them achieve the things that God has put in their hearts to do.

As their pastor, I also want to make sure that their marriages are healthy and their finances are in order. Their health is everything to the life of the church. They have to be an example and demonstration of authentic Christianity. Nancy and I have to model this for them and continually remind them of how important it is for them to be people who are continually maturing as disciples themselves.

GUIDELINES FOR THE CIRCLES

When the Lord gave me this idea to implement, we were already well into the development of our church. You might be thinking to yourself, "There is no way I could change the culture of my church with an idea like this!" But let me encourage you by sharing that we made these changes after our church had grown to over 700 weekly attendees. I asked each and every current leader to lead by example and attend our new Vineyard 101 course.

In helping guide the culture of your church, you must be wary of allowing shortcuts. To the degree to which you stay firm to your leadership principles is to the degree to which it can transform your leadership culture.

Here are some guidelines that are important to abide by when implementing a similar cultural shift among your leadership team:

1. It is essential that no leader skips circles.

You cannot invite someone into leadership from the first circle. It is important to have people be a disciple first before they are given the responsibility of being a discipler. This quickly becomes a humility filter for the church. You will know who is willing to be led and who is simply striving for position.

When people begin attending your church from other churches and have previously served in high levels of leadership, it is a challenge to see their gifting and not immediately put them into leadership roles. This does not happen at Vineyard Boise. I ask everyone to go to our Vineyard 101 class. I do this because I want them to catch our vision, to partake in our culture, and to participate in our structure.

I have seen churches that take people out of the first circle and make them elders. Personally, I will not take resumes from people who want jobs and staff positions at our church. I have a deep conviction that if I want to build a community of love and trust, the people must grow up through this system. Our values and vision are more caught than taught. Some people will tell me, "But that is already me." But unless they are living in the midst of the culture, they can't really understand it. To this day, every pastor on our staff has passed through this system.

2. "Build slow to go fast."

As your church begins to grow and build for the future, many

of the problems you currently have will disappear. In a larger congregation, people will give up on trying to make you the pastor
that they want you to be. (I'm sure
many of you will find this to be a great
relief!) But it is hard to stand your
ground on leadership when others are
begging you to change. If you know
God has called you to a specific vision,
don't be swayed by people who want to
change it. Bowing to every different
request in the church will only cause
chaos within your church culture. And
if you do change for a specific person, you never know if that person will be around when the sun comes up.

> If you know God has
> called you to a specific
> vision, don't be swayed
> by people who want to
> change it.

I remember people telling me in the early stages of our
church, "I'll die with you. I'm your man. I'll be with you for as
long as the church is here." But the minute there was any kind of
hiccup in the church, or the second that I asked that person to do
something that was uncomfortable for them, they were gone.
Instilling a culture that revolves around steadfast values within the
model of discipleship can help discern between the talkers and the
doers. Our circle process shows us who is tenacious and is going
to stick around, which is far more important to me than gifting.

John Wimber always said, "Build slow to go fast." One of the things that our circle process forces us to do is go slow. You do not want to get ahead of yourself. You do not want to get excited about someone and lay hands on him or her too soon (an important biblical concept). It is easy to lay hands on someone, but hard to take your hands off. Other pastors of large congregations have told me the same thing time and again: Firing a prominent staff member can sometimes set the church growth back for two years. It is important to carefully consider your staff selections in those early stages of church growth.

As leaders, we sometimes find ourselves in the position Samuel did when he went to anoint King Saul's successor. Samuel looked at Jesse's sons and thought he could pick out the next king by how they looked. We can have a difficult time ignoring the outside (as God does) and looking directly at the heart. But at Vineyard Boise, with our values coming from the top down and people's involvement being measured and monitored on the way up, it is extremely difficult to advance into leadership without having the right heart.

The Supportive Structure

Managing a Teamwork Matrix

We have all been there, mediating a tense meeting between two people with very different viewpoints and goals for the church. One person believes the purpose of the church is to accomplish specific tasks (like the Great Commission). The other person believes the purpose of the church is to develop meaningful relationships (as Jesus did with His disciples). Trying to get these two groups of people to work together can make you want to pull all your hair out. Perhaps your own personal bent makes you favor one group over the other, making you wish the group less like you would go away. But the truth is we need each viewpoint in the church. We especially need this diversity in our leadership teams. It is helpful to remember this issue is something Jesus dealt with in His ministry.

As Jesus and the disciples continued on their way to Jerusalem, they came to a village where a woman named Martha welcomed them into her home. Her sister, Mary, sat at the Lord's feet, listening to what he taught. But Martha was worrying over the big dinner she was preparing. She came to Jesus and said, "Lord, doesn't it seem unfair to you that my sister just sits here while I do all the work? Tell her to come and help me." But the Lord said to her, "My dear Martha, you are so upset over all these details! There is really only one thing worth being concerned about. Mary has discovered it – and I won't take it away from her."

— LUKE 10:38-42

Yes, the Marys and the Marthas. And we need both of them to accomplish all that God has called us to do. Pressing into relationships is important, especially in the realm of our relationship with Christ. But like James warns us, faith without works is dead (James 2:17). We cannot forget the work that must be done. So we must be able to strike a balance between these two mindsets that results in a transforming fellowship of believers, rooted in love and trust. So, how do we do this? The answer for Vineyard Boise has been found in a carefully defined structure.

THE ROLE OF STRUCTURE IN SYNERGY

Our final piece of the synergy triangle is structure. No matter how much vision you impart or how much culture you develop, without structure the work of the church will struggle to maintain consistent momentum. As we implement structure into our churches, we construct a framework upon which we can resource our people so they can efficiently accomplish our God-given vision. This includes establishing plans, programs, management systems, leadership development, facilities, schedules, calendars, and events.

Whenever structure is implemented in a church, there can be both benefits and deficits. One of the positive elements of structure is that it helps keep efficiency levels up and frustration levels down. For instance, it would be very frustrating for a church if their pastor encouraged them to serve the poor, yet had no structure in place to facilitate them doing so. Structure also can build lines of communication that help everyone stay focused and on task. Other benefits of structure include the following:

• Good administration uses the right people in the right places at the right times.

• Good organization clarifies lines of authority.

• Good structure helps stretch money and resources because it demands budgeting up front and accountability later.

• Good organization develops only the programs that are helpful to accomplish the vision.

• Good organization and administration save time and energy, preventing needless burnout.

- Good organization builds the right facilities that will encompass and enhance the vision.
- Good organization looks to the future and plans for it.

Perhaps the most exciting news concerning structure is that, when used correctly, it promotes freedom.

If you have administrative skills as part of your leadership skill set (a "Martha" pastor), you are probably reading this with a triumphant fist in the air, saying to yourself, "I knew it!" If you are more relational in the way you lead (a "Mary" pastor), you might be terrified thinking how constricting a structure can be. But relax; structure gives us a framework within which to work effectively, giving us freedom in our ministry. In fact, with a good structure in place, you will find yourself freer to do the things you always wanted to do but never found the time to do.

There are also deficits that may crop up as a result of structure. This is not to discourage you, but to make you aware so you can deal with these issues if they arise. Some of these problems include:

- Too much organization can cause a church to fall into a routine.
- Too much structuring can cause people to serve the organization instead of the organism.
- Too much structure can stifle freedom and discourage the

creative thinking that birthed the church in the first place.

- Too much structure can squelch spontaneity and the ability to challenge the status quo.
- Too much structure can cause over-cautiousness and prohibit risk taking, creating confinement to the rules.
- Too much structure can make us become codified or systematic in our approach to ministry.

Finding the right type and amount of structure may seem overwhelming. There are hundreds of ideas about how to structure churches, many of which lead us right into the fears about structure that we have had all along. Too much structure will hinder our creativity and freedom; not enough structure will lead to disarray and chaos in trying to accomplish our vision. Striking a balance in developing a structure is crucial to finding the right one. For some good guidelines in discovering and defining this structure, let's return to our clash between Mary and Martha.

THE MARYS AND THE MARTHAS

I find the analogy of Mary and Martha extremely relevant in helping form a structure that benefits the entire church. The Mary group consists of highly relational people. They are people who are not very concerned with programming or getting specific tasks done. What brings the most joy to their lives is hanging out with people and ministering to them. For the most part, they are pastoral in nature, and they love to be in the presence of the Lord as well as the presence of other people. If you asked a person from the Mary group what the purpose of the church is, they might say it is all about building relationships with God and other people.

The Martha group consists of task-oriented people. They are the people who say the church needs to bear fruit, accomplish certain goals, pray regularly, evangelize the lost, go to the mission field, serve the poor, and counsel the broken. While they may enjoy relationships, nothing drives them more than seeing certain tasks completed by the church. If you asked a person from the Martha group what the purpose of the church is, they might say that it is all about building the Kingdom of God.

What I have observed over the years is there are Mary churches and there are Martha churches, depending upon the leaning of the senior pastor. Some pastors are more Mary in their makeup, deferring to their gifting in the realm of relationships and pastoral ministry. They tend to focus on those issues more so than others. Other pastors are more Martha in their nature, wanting to build the Kingdom and get the job done.

It is my belief that we need both Marys and Marthas. They are sisters who live together and must work together. As I recognized this need for teamwork within our church, I developed a structured system which I felt was necessary to encourage and enforce interdependence in my leadership team. That system has come to be known as the "matrix" system.

THE BLUE PILL OR THE RED PILL?

Because of the Matrix movie trilogy, we tend to have this warped view of what a matrix really is. You may think of Keanu Reeves and choosing between a red pill and a blue pill. Or you may think of the matrix as something that is extremely static and structural. The actual definition of the word "matrix" is "a situation or surrounding substance within which something else originates, develops, or is contained" or "the womb." That's how we see the matrix at our church; it's a place that develops ministry and brings life to the church.

With the matrix, we have been able to neutralize two of the most damaging attitudes that can exist among the leadership of the church: independence and co-dependence. When you have a leader who firmly believe in his total independence, you have someone who has his own ideas and does not want anyone to interfere with his ministry or what he is doing. He has all the answers for his ministry (and maybe a few answers for others). There are also co-dependent leaders who stifle the life on their teams because they micromanage every detail, exerting too much control.

For the church to really flourish and function, it needs to be interdependent. A church of interdependent people consists of those who love each other and are willing to work with one another. This type of attitude is especially critical if you're trying to build a community of love that is truly functional. Within this structure, you will have the relational elements and the fruit bearing ones as well.

It is our desire at Vineyard Boise to meld these two ideas together – bringing structure to our church that would accomplish our God-given vision and serve the culture emerging from it.

UNDERSTANDING THE MATRIX

The matrix system consists of a grid with a horizontal and vertical axis, which helps us visualize what true interdependence looks like among the leadership of the church.

Let's study the diagram on the following page.

STRUCTURE Matrix

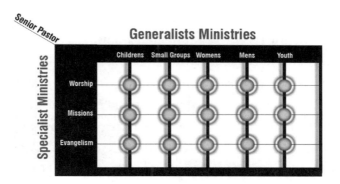

The horizontal axis consists of the Mary-type ministries – the pastoral and relational styles of ministry. These are the "people group" ministries. For example, the children's ministry falls under the Mary group. The heart of the children's pastor is to disciple the children and to have relationship with them, helping them mature and grow into authentic followers of Christ. The youth ministry, the men's ministry, the women's ministry, the small group ministry – they are all what we call "generalist" ministries, or relational ministries, which fall on the horizontal axis of the matrix grid.

The vertical axis consists of the Martha-type ministries – the task-oriented styles of ministry. For example, the worship ministry falls under the Martha group. The worship director's heart should be to provide every ministry in the church with the opportunity to enter into worship. Evangelism, missions, prayer, benevolence, counseling, curriculum development – they are all what we call "specialist" ministries, or task-oriented ministries, which fall on the vertical axis of the matrix grid.

If you ask worship leaders if they are a Mary or a Martha in their approach to ministry, most will respond that they are a Mary. They will say things like, "I just want to sit at the Lord's feet and worship." But that is not altogether true. Granted, there definitely has to be some Mary in those leaders, but most worship leaders are very focused on tweaking sound systems, putting together good worship teams, building a good worship set, and bringing the church to a place of worship – all Martha in their focus. They are not as concerned with missions or evangelism because their real passion is to worship the Lord and help the entire church worship as well. The worship leader feels 90 percent of the church budget should be used for sound equipment and instruments.

Another Martha ministry is evangelism. Someone who has the heart of an evangelist feels that the whole purpose of the church is to win the lost to Christ. Evangelism directors feel that 90 percent of the budget should be used for outreach and evangelism. Their passion is to share their faith with others and help equip others to do so as well.

Then, you have the Martha ministry of missions. The missions pastor says if Christians are not going to other nations, then they are not truly fulfilling the call of God on their lives. Their whole focus is on bringing the Gospel to other people groups. Like their previous two counterparts, the missions director feels 90 percent of the budget should be used to take the Gospel to the ends of the Earth.

How do you help bring balance to each one of these passionate ministry leaders? After all, they are all right. We do need to worship. We need to share our faith. We need to play a part in missions, both locally and abroad. But we are also called to serve the poor, to counsel the broken, to pray corporately. Ultimately, we find that each leader brings an important aspect of church life to the table.

Trying to get all of these ministries to work together has given many senior pastors huge headaches and sleepless nights. The matrix system eliminates the guesswork and helps clearly define the way in which both generalist and specialist ministries will partner together to further the vision of the church.

For example, in many churches the worship director believes his primary job is to lead worship for the weekend church services. However, the matrix system creates a more complete job description for them. As each horizontal line of generalist ministries (such as men's ministry, women's ministry, small groups, youth ministry, and children's ministry) pass through the vertical lines of the specialist ministries (such as worship, missions, or evangelism), new responsibilities are created at each intersection. On the matrix grid, as worship intersects with children's ministry, the worship director becomes responsible to see that the children's ministry has a competent worship leader. As worship intersects with the youth ministry, the worship director has the responsibility of assembling and raising up a good band for the youth. And down the horizontal line it goes. With the matrix in place, providing worship through the entire horizontal plane becomes the worship director's job. The worship director wants to help the whole church worship, not just the adults on Sunday morning.

By the same token, the evangelism director should have a similar heart, not to create an independent or isolated department of evangelism, but that the value of evangelism would penetrate every person participating in generalist ministries. Instead of planning evangelism events for just a few people who feel called to it, the evangelism leaders should desire that the children would understand evangelism and have the tools to evangelize their own age group. As their vertical line intersects with each generalist ministry, they should have a desire to equip, train, and provide opportunity and resources for evangelism at each intersection. They should help the youth with tools and teaching in order to equip them to influence their peers for Christ. And the evang ism director should do the same with the college and career age group, the men's ministry, the women's ministry, the small groups, etc. All of those generalist ministries should have not only an expression of worship, but also an expression of evangelism.

Much like the worship director must find worship leaders for each ministry, the evangelism leader must find someone already within each generalist ministry who shares a heart for evangelism and invite those people to be on the evangelism task force. The evangelism leader recruits someone from each generalist ministry to help lead and direct evangelism within those ministries, consequently impacting the entire church.

BECOME A CHURCH OF ALL EXPRESSIONS
OF THE GOSPEL

As the matrix system begins to take shape throughout the ministries of the church, the impact will leave you with a community that will never be the same. I believe the matrix system pays high dividends by creating a dynamic community. For instance, take the average small group leader. These people are most likely lay leaders. They work full-time jobs, come home tired like everyone else, and try to shape a handful of people into authentic disciples of Christ. If a member of their group enters the hospital, they will visit them. If somebody in their group needs food, they will find a way to provide them with all the meals they need. They build life-changing relationships with their people. They are highly pastoral in their giftings and very "Mary" in their makeup.

However, for a disciple to become authentic in his faith, he needs to understand how to worship, how to share his faith, how to take his faith to people abroad, and how to pray. Sometimes small group leaders will find themselves in counseling situations where they need more skills and resources than what is personally available to them. The average small group leader would not only be lacking in time but also in ideas to help make some of these vital components of discipleship meaningful and available to his small group. This is where the specialist ministers can come alongside the generalist ministry leaders, providing the resources needed for the full expression of the Christian experience.

At Vineyard Boise, this type of injection of specialist help into our generalist ministries empowers and affords everyone the opportunity to experience the full expression of the church body. For example, consider our benevolence ministry which has a vision to take care of the poor. In our church, like many others, there is a small group of people who have a heart to care for the poor. If they did all the work themselves, they would be limited by their own capacity. But with the matrix system, the benevolence director provides opportunities for all the generalist ministries to reach out to the poor. They go to the youth and train them to work in the food pantry. They coach the college age group on how to work among the homeless. They equip small groups, mobilizing them to go out and do some type of ministry among the poor. Now the benevolence director not only has a vision for the benevolence ministry, but they have a whole church participating with them to see it accomplished.

Every Sunday afternoon following our morning services, we have a barbecue for the homeless in Boise. The benevolence ministry organizes that event by gathering the equipment and food. They then go to our church's small groups and say, "Will you come serve with us twice a year on a Sunday afternoon?" If small groups agree, we have more than enough people to throw a barbecue every single week.

One of the major advantages to the matrix is it is an effective tool against having a burned-out congregation. Instead of feeling guilty about asking the few "doers" in a church to do another thing, pastors begin opening up areas of service among the entire church. With new people being given the opportunity to participate, the people who have tried to manage ministries on their own shoulders will no longer experience burn out.

Other advantages of the matrix include the following:

- People are no longer isolated in one ministry as they become familiar with different ministries and interact with new groups of people.

- The church does not become dominated by programs.
- The church does not become departmentalized, as each department now interacts with each another, all working together for the common good and a common vision.
- People do not experience just one expression of the Christian life but become well-rounded as they grow in their faith.

BUILDING A NET

In the early days of the Vineyard Movement, the leadership stressed the importance of "building a net to catch the harvest." The necessity of nets still remains. In order to integrate new followers of Christ into our church, we must have a way to accomplish healthy assimilation. I believe the matrix system serves as that net. It is a network of many people working together to accomplish the main goals and vision of the church.

Every time a horizontal and vertical line intersects, it creates a job or a place for a person to participate. Steve Sjogren, a well-known Vineyard pastor, once told me the best way to grow a church is to provide opportunities for everyone. He said if you give them all responsibilities, they will not be as likely to leave. And the matrix provides hundreds of jobs! At every intersection, there is another place to play. As new people commit their lives to

Christ, our church has a way to connect them to service, providing opportunities for them to deepen their faith as they serve God. By providing dozens of opportunities, we have done something that is absolutely necessary in building community – we have made people feel valued, needed, and wanted.

DEFINING ACCOUNTABILITY WITHIN THE MATRIX

In examining the matrix, one question that always arises is this: How do you determine who each team member reports to? Let's consider a fictional worship leader for the youth group, who we will call Jim. Jim has two overseers: both the worship director and the youth pastor. So, who does Jim go to when he has an issue to resolve? Who holds Jim accountable for his position? Jim's true passion rests in worship, but he also loves relating to young people. Most of all, he likes to help the youth engage in worship. At a cursory glance, it appears as though Jim's allegiances are divided between the two passions and between his two overseers. Which ministry is he really serving?

A closer examination of the matrix system answers Jim's angst with ease. For issues that are more pastoral, Jim would go to the youth pastor. This is what he would do if, in his interaction with the youth, he found one of them doing drugs and tempting other teens. For issues that are more task-oriented, such as Jim having difficulty with his drummer keeping rhythm during the worship set, he would meet with the worship director. Likewise, if there were an issue with Jim on a pastoral level, such as dishonoring God with his lifestyle, then the youth pastor would speak to Jim about it. And if there were a task-oriented issue, such as Jim's inability to play the guitar and sing at the same time, then the worship pastor would speak to him about this.

When there are overarching issues with Jim, both the youth pastor and the worship director come together, providing Jim with accountability and challenging him to do his job with greater competence. Ultimately, both the youth pastor and the worship director need to be on the same page, of one heart and one mind, in their jobs of discipling Jim.

HELPING YOU MANAGE AS YOU GROW

After reading all of this, you may be saying to yourself, "This sounds like a great idea, but I just have a church plant. I am lucky if I have someone to play guitar on Sunday morning, much less a children's pastor, a youth pastor, a missions director, a benevolence leader, or a counselor on staff with me." Don't worry. The matrix system is adaptable for you as well and contains the necessary flexibility to grow with you. Regardless of the size of the church, the matrix system enables you to implement a management system that does not need major reconstruction every time you experience a growth spurt.

Oftentimes when using other management structures, the whole system has to be torn down in order to build up for the next level of ministry. As we have put the matrix system to work for us, the beauty of it has been how it continues to grow on both the horizontal and vertical planes. When a church is first planted, it has a senior pastor on the corner of the matrix (we'll talk more about the senior pastor's role in just a bit). There may also be a worship leader and possibly someone who has a heart for the children, and, if you want to stretch it a little bit, maybe even some small group leaders. If that's all you have, then you have worship on your vertical plane. And then you have a few ministries on the horizontal plane (see diagram below).

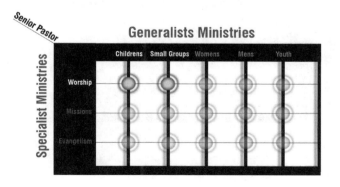

That is a good place to begin. At the very least, you know what you've got. You simply prompt the worship leader to work together with those budding generalist ministries. As a result, the worship leader will discover new worship talent among the weekly attendees and it will empower them to grow the worship team.

As the church grows and develops, it is possible that you will develop a youth, men's and women's ministry, and you begin to place those on the grid as well. Suddenly, the system begins expanding with the church (see diagram below).

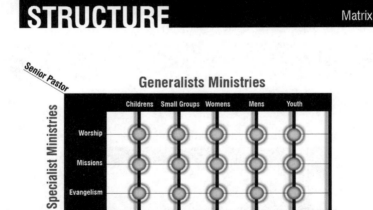

Another memorable piece of ministry advice Steve Sjogram gave me was this: "Always have three available jobs that need people. At least then you know what you need and what to recruit for." So, if you have a need in your matrix for someone to lead your prayer ministry, counseling ministry or ministry to the poor, list those ministries on the vertical plane of the matrix because they are your church's values, even though you may not have a leader ready to take that position.

It is important to understand as you are setting up the matrix system for your church that the specialist ministries clearly represent your core values as a church. Do you value worship? Then worship needs to be a specialist ministry. Do you value missions? Then missions needs to be a specialist ministry. Do you value outreach? Then evangelism and benevolence need to be listed as specialist ministries. Even though you may not start with all of the people in place, you at least have created the framework in your church for continued growth.

> The matrix itself is a visual job description that shows each leader exactly what they are to do.

Next, you start praying for God to send people to your church to help take up those values. Once these people show up, they will immediately recognize what their job will be. The matrix itself is a visual job description that shows each leader exactly what they are to do.

THE SENIOR PASTOR'S ROLE

In looking at the matrix system, you may be scratching your head, wondering where the senior pastor belongs in this structure. The senior pastor's job description has changed somewhat and has become better defined by the matrix. The senior pastor sits on the corner of the matrix, taking on the large task of working with both generalist and specialist ministry leaders and encouraging the two groups to work together.

As the church grows and develops, a senior pastor may also need an administrative pastor who sits with the senior pastor on the corner of the matrix and oversees the management responsibility, coordinating the budgets and the events that happen among the ministries. The senior pastor's role then shifts slightly to become the spiritual and inspirational overseer of the entire matrix.

When you lay the matrix up against the leadership circle described in the last chapter, you will find that the generalist and specialist ministry leaders are all in the fourth circle. These are the people who develop ministry all throughout the church. They are leaders of leaders. These leaders are the primary responsibility of the senior pastor.

Quietly, a senior pastor works his way out of many job reduces it to one. As the senior pastor develops leaders, such as a counseling director, then the senior pastor does little or no counseling himself, which gives him more time to raise up other leaders. As the senior pastor discovers someone to take on the missions ministry, the senior pastor no longer has to make decisions about how the mission money is spent and where mission efforts are directed. Instead, the missions director has his own task force that makes those decisions for the church.

The senior pastor sits on the outside of the matrix, motivating, encouraging, resourcing, and providing whatever is needed as he serves the leaders in the matrix. He sits on the corner, coordinating the Marys and the Marthas, continually encouraging them to work together and to respond to each other. This is often difficult since their inclination is to not work with one another. Task people and relational people don't always see eye-to-eye. But it is the senior pastor's responsibility to see that they work closely together and resolve whatever problems are taking place within the matrix grid itself.

WARNING: BE PATIENT

One thing I discovered as I implemented this matrix system into my leadership team was that everyone thought it was a great idea on paper, but it took three years to bring it to fruition. I found it really exposed independence and codependence on our team. People would say they wanted to be team players, but had trouble doing it. There were some leaders who could not exist in the matrix, and eventually I lost them. The leaders who replaced them were team players. They were interdependent, liked the input of others, and thrived in the teamwork environment.

When I first brought the matrix system before our leadership team, everybody had an "aha" moment when they thought it was a good idea. But implementing it was hard work. When we first began using this system, we had a grid in our meeting room, giving us a visual reminder of how this system worked. But now that teamwork has become a part of our culture, we do not have to have a physical matrix grid in front of us. Now we just say we are going to "matrix this" or "matrix that," meaning our specialist and generalist ministries will work together to build ministries throughout the church. Matrix is a more of a philosophical way of working together. I would warn any pastor not to try to use this as a static management tool. Not every ministry fits into the matrix system; trying to force it would be a mistake.

The matrix system is a fluid, living thing. Making it become rigid will result in frustration on the senior pastor's part and team members will find it difficult to work together. However, if implemented with care and precision, senior pastors can find themselves enjoying their favorite elements of pastoral ministry, free from management hassles that often dominate their time.

Leadership

Having the Heart
of a Synergistic Leader

Thinking about this final section, I became aware of the quality and effectiveness of our leadership team at Vineyard Boise. It is my heart to paint a picture for you of the life of a church that is in pursuit of synergistic leadership.

This past weekend was the second weekend in February and also Valentine's Day. As a result, it was a bit more hectic than normal. Besides our regular weekend services, I counted 10 other major events that took place between Friday and Sunday nights.

The weekend began with an elaborate Renaissance Valentine's Dinner that served a catered meal and provided fun entertainment to 140 married couples on Friday evening. At the same time, another ministry team was serving dinner to 100 people at our "Celebrate Recovery" ministry. In a third area of the same building, a group of leaders was participating in a teaching intensive through the Vineyard Leadership Institute. As usual, these events were supported by a team of childcare workers ministering to the children of these participants.

Also happening that weekend, around 50 junior high students with a plethora of leaders, loaded into vans for their annual winter camp. Another group known as "Rachel's Vineyard" was beginning a weekend retreat for the purpose of healing men and woman from the devastating repercussions of abortion.

After extensive cleanup and re-set on Saturday morning, our main building facilitated three more leadership training events.

On Sunday following multiple services for adults, youth, children, and pre-school, the facility was prepared for yet another major outreach event called "Operation Deployed Valentine." This was a catered dinner for those in our community whose spouses are serving overseas in military service. This event ministered to families outside our own church but required 140 volunteer workers to pull it off. It not only involved serving a formal dinner, but providing hospitality, relevant speakers, extensive childcare, set-up and clean up.

This may all sound quite exhausting, but because Vineyard Boise is full of synergistic leaders, no one was stressed out or overworked, and every event was more than successful.

Although Nancy and I attended two of the dinners, we had no responsibility except to be participants. A few things occurred to me as I sat and proudly watched our leaders in action. One was how many lay leaders and trained volunteers it required to pull off the weekend's events. Another observation was how much fun the volunteers were having and how much satisfaction they received for their involvement. To my great joy, I noticed none of our paid staff had up-front parts in any of the major events. For example, I watched as Tempe McFarlane, our Community Outreach Director, stood on the sidelines as her team did all the forefront work, including speaking at the Operation Deployed Valentine banquet. It also occurred to me that one of our Elder couples, Joe and Janet Ingrao, had overseen four of the 10 events that weekend. Yet, like me, their only role was to show up and encourage the people who were directly responsible. Although attending four major events plus participating in Sunday morning services over the course of three days is a load for any leader, the Ingraos were elated and rewarded by the effectiveness of the people they had identified and trained for these key leadership roles.

In our staff meeting the following Tuesday, the sharing went on for an hour about all that had transpired during those few days. The spirit of synergy empowered us and energized us to prepare for yet another week of ministry.

As I look back on that busy weekend, I am not only thankful, but also very aware that the life and ministry taking place at Vineyard Boise is due in large part to the synergistic leadership of my staff and the leaders they have gathered around them.

SEVEN QUALITIES OF A SYNERGISTIC LEADER

Becoming a synergistic leader is not so much a strategic change as an issue of the heart. Let's look at seven qualities of a synergistic leader:

1. The synergistic leader has the heart of a scout.

The synergistic leader is one who has made a life habit of scouting for potential new leaders. Nearly every leadership book I have read poses the question, "Are leaders born or made?" My response has always been "Yes." In my observation, great leaders are like gifted artists; while they possess natural gifting that can only come from above, they have a motivated desire to grow and learn transferable skills. The great leaders I have encountered through the years all possessed certain inner qualities that launched them on the leadership journey. But it was the influence and training of other great leaders that allowed their God-given gifting to be fanned into culture changing flames. The synergistic leader must be on a constant search for people who not only have natural gifting and passion but also possess a heart to be raised up and trained for specific roles. The heart of a synergistic leader is one that is not only unthreatened by the gifting in these potential leaders, but eagerly embraces people who possess the abilities to take the church to higher levels of effectiveness.

2. The synergetic leader experiences the most satisfaction when those they are leading succeed.

Synergistic leaders are like parents who love to see their kids succeed. They are leaders who experience the greatest fulfillment when those they have raised up excel. I grew up watching my father lead. He has a PhD in administrative education and was the principal of Beverly Hills High School for 18 years. His role was considered one of the most prestigious in public education at that time. When I was a young boy, he used to give me pointers on how to succeed in life. I remember him telling me there were two different ways to climb a ladder. He told me some leaders aggressively fight their way over all those on the lower rungs, stepping on and climbing over as many people as possible until the top is finally achieved. On the other hand, he said there are some leaders who would encourage and even physically help the people around them climb upward until everyone is on the top. He would end his story with a question like, "Who do you think will be the happiest and the most fulfilled when they arrive at the top?" or, "Which leader would you like to follow?" The synergistic leader is the leader who gets personal satisfaction in the success of others. They are leaders who are more concerned with seeing people blessed and empowered in the process of fulfilling the vision than the achievement of the task itself. Personal recognition is of less importance than the accomplishments of the victorious team.

,. The synergistic leader can balance servanthood and godly ambition.

The synergistic leader must walk the fine line between others-centered servanthood and the zeal to get things done. Once when I was mustering up the courage to apply for my first real job as a line boy at our local municipal airport, my father told me another story. It went something like this: Two young men were waiting for an interview with a future employer. As the first young man was invited into the office, the employer casually asked him to close the door. The young man turned and gently closed the door and took his seat. A short time later, the second young man was invited in and the request was repeated. This young man turned and closed the office door, then noticing an open closet door and nearby cabinet door, he quickly closed them as well. Before taking his seat, he turned to the amazed employer and said, "Are there any more doors that need to be closed, sir?" Again my father asked the obvious question: "Which man do you think got the job?" After all these years, I've never forgotten the point of that story and have continually tried to balance a servant leadership style with godly ambition. Leaders must first be servants, but there must be a level of aggressiveness and eagerness to get things done. The synergistic leader is a person who has learned to walk in this delicate balance. I have met people who somehow felt it was wrong to ask God for success. I love how Nehemiah ended his prayer of intercession for the reconstruction of Jerusalem. He prayed, "Please grant me success now as I go to ask the king for a great favor" (Nehemiah 1:11). He knew that if he were not successful in speaking to the king of Persia his dream to restore the city would never get off the ground. Vision is a verb; it not only requires faith to believe for the impossible, but proactive action as well.

4. Synergistic leadership requires tenacity and stick-to-itiveness.

If the synergistic leader truly believes in where he is going, he will be tenacious in getting there. My father always told me the key to successful leadership is doing just a little more than the other guy. He would then add with a twinkle in his eye, "… and that generally isn't a lot." He would say the key to getting ahead in life is to simply keep showing up. Synergistic leadership requires tenacity and stick-to-itiveness. If the Lord has given the leader authentic vision, then that vision will produce a driving force that will energize the leader's motivations for years to come. This is necessary because developing healthy culture is a continuous and never-ending undertaking.

5. Synergistic leadership requires trust and trustworthiness.

The synergistic leader must earn the trust of those they expect

.ow them. Trust is a quality that is developed over time.

; said, "Whoever can be trusted with very little can also be ιι.ʌsted with much, and whoever is dishonest with very little will also be dishonest with much. So if you have not been trustworthy in handling worldly wealth, who will trust you with true riches? And if you have not been trustworthy with someone else's property, who will give you property of your own?" (Luke 16:10-12). When training new leaders it is essential to explain the importance of trust.

Using **TRUST** as an acronym, we can illuminate its five most important principles.

T – Truth lived out. When we have received Biblical truth into our lives, the fruit of the Holy Spirit begin to flow out of us (love, joy, peace, patience, kindness, goodness, faithfulness, gentleness and self-control - Galatians 5:22-23) and we become trustworthy.

R – Repentance & reconciliation. Trust occurs when we, in humility, take ownership for our mistakes and are able to admit we are wrong. We become trustworthy only after we have allowed God to heal us from our woundedness.

U – Understanding. We will only trust those we feel care about us and truly understand us.

S – Servanthood & stability. We trust those we feel are not self-serving. Servanthood is the signature of love. Jesus said He

did not come to be served, but to serve. Likewise, stabi.
essential ingredient in trust because we trust those we kn
spiritually and emotionally stable.

T – Time tested. Trust is earned over time. Concerning the
leadership role of a deacon, Paul said, "Before they are appointed
as deacons, they should be given other responsibilities in the
church as a test of their character and ability. If they do well, then
they may serve as deacons" (1 Timothy 3:10).

The synergistic leader must be one who has over time earned
the trust of those who will follow them due to their long term
record of integrity and authenticity. *Ldshp.*

6. **The synergistic leader must be a structural engineer.** *exp.*

The synergistic leader must have the skills to create structure
for maintaining healthy church growth and culture. One of the
downfalls of the Jesus Movement of the 1970s was its negative
attitude towards anything that smacked of "the establishment."
The Jesus movement was birthed in rebellion against the established church. As is often the case with overreaction, it swung to
the opposite extreme having little or no emphasis on structure.
Organization was held suspect as a sign of not being directed by
the spontaneity of the Holy Spirit. Structure of any kind was of
little value, even in a physical sense. Churches gathered in store-
fronts and warehouse facilities instead of traditional church buildings. Children's ministries focused more on the necessity of child-

care than on deliberate educational activity because "Sunday school" was seen as a structured program of the past. Churches grew in the charismatic excitement that birthed them, but over time, many collapsed like houses built without proper framework.

For the culture to thrive and the vision to advance, church leadership must provide integrity in budgeting, long range planning, defined managements systems, clear lines of communication and strategic training. Of all the ingredients necessary to become a synergistic leader, organizational skills are the easiest to learn. While vision can only come from above and culture is evasive and abstract, structure is tangible and teachable. Paul tells us that leadership is a grace gift of the Father saying, "If God has given you leadership ability, take the responsibility seriously..." (Romans 12:8). Of all the skills necessary to lead, it has been my observation that administration is the most attainable through training. Synergistic leaders must have a heart of humility that will motivate them to grow in the skills that might otherwise hold back the ministries they are endeavoring to build.

7. Synergistic leadership is chemistry in action.

The synergistic leader innately understands how to mix the inactive ingredients of individual gifting into a substance of explosive reaction. Synergistic leadership knows how to empower and bring harmony to the unique gifting found in a community of believers. It is a leadership style that recognizes that individual gifting, standing on its own, will have limited impact. However, when these gifts are integrated together, a group of believers can accomplish the impossible. The synergistic leader recognizes that the ingredients of vision, culture, and structure are like the independent parts of epoxy glue. Isolated and alone, they have little value, but together they provide a powerful force that impacts all it touches.

Another Revolution

Increasing Momentum

I n the previous sections, we have taken the first lap around the synergy cycle. We have closely examined the elements of vision, culture, and structure and have learned how one influences the other. We have seen that leaders must ignite these three spark plugs to move forward in power and effectiveness, building momentum as they go.

We have also discovered each of these plugs must fire in their sequential order – first vision, then culture, and finally the supporting structure. If they fire out of order, a backfire can occur causing the forward momentum to stall.

It is not uncommon for pastors wanting to kick start momentum in their church to search for a program to ignite the dwindling spark. They may bring another's vision back to their church, selling it to the people as new vision, in hopes it will stimulate the culture. In this case, it is not vision but program, and thus structure. Because people innately know the difference between true vision and a program, the introduction of the new idea may be perceived by the culture as counterfeit. Remember, structure can only support what God-given vision is already doing in the culture. If the structure is sold as vision, it will usually backfire. If it is introduced as structure to support a struggling culture, at the right time and in the right way, it will enhance it. But this is a delicate balance and requires the attentiveness of a leader sensitive to the needs of his people. He must exercise wisdom, understanding the importance of perfect timing. This is synergistic leadership.

Let me emphasize, too little or too much structure can be equally damaging. It is very important that there is no misunderstanding of this principle concerning the use of new programs; there are some wonderful and effective programs out there that can support your culture – if you use them in the right way at the right time. Programs such as Rick Warren's "40 Days of Purpose," or the international evangelism program "Alpha," have proven time and again to enhance the life of most churches. Though we use many proven programs at Vineyard Boise, we understand they are not the vision, merely structural tools to meet the changing needs in a culture intent on growing disciples.

Also, remember that not only do the spark plugs of vision, culture, and structure need to fire in sequence, but they must fire over and over again. Every revolution of the synergy cycle must revisit the vision, tweak the culture, and adjust the structure. Then you will continue to build momentum.

GOING AROUND AGAIN

Recently I felt the conviction of the Holy Spirit regarding the church's overall neglect of God's creation. I felt the Lord directing us towards the area of environmental stewardship, and that He would use this arena to draw hundreds of new people to Himself. I knew this would be a sensitive issue, as most people perceive care of the environment to be part of the liberal agenda. Though I realized this was a false perception, it was a powerful force that must not be overlooked.

I also knew that for real change to take place, I had to follow the synergy cycle. God put a new vision in my heart and I had to prepare to sell it in a way that it would become a part of our culture.

Like Nehemiah, I gathered an inner circle of expertise (Nehemiah 2). I quietly built a taskforce of people from our church who worked in environmental fields such as soil conservation, National Parks Department, Fish and Game Department, and so on. This team helped me build a strategy, and with this strategy, I addressed the church during the weekend services. Using the Nehemiah model, I sold the vision with as much conviction as I could. Preaching a message titled "Let's Tend the Garden," I challenged our people to embrace this very important aspect of stewardship. The church gave a standing ovation and the

. entered our culture. As Nehemiah put it, "We immediately began this good work." At those services, I announced an environmental stewardship meeting for the following week that everyone was welcome to attend. At that meeting, we presented all the ways people could participate. We offered a list of seminars, recycling plans, community service projects, and wilderness trail building opportunities. We provided a structure to support the excitement that was present in the culture. We were off and running. Each corner of the synergy cycle was addressed, and environmental stewardship became a normal part of our life as a church.

REVOLUTIONARY QUESTIONS

As I mentioned before, every year we have a leadership meeting where I gather my top leaders (Circle 4 leaders) and take them away for a few days for debriefing and planning. We review our past year, asking ourselves some basic questions:

1. Did we make progress on our vision this year? Did we effectively communicate the vision; was it clear to everyone?

Habakkuk 2:2 tells us that we are to write the vision on tablets in large, clear letters so all the people can read it and run with it [Living Bible]. When I am consulting with pastors who are struggling with their churches, I often ask them if their people really know where they are trying to take them. If there is hesitancy in responding, it is generally because the pastor does not clearly know where they are going. If I have the opportunity, I will ask the same question of this pastor's leaders. Do they know the vision the pastor has for the church and how it is being accomplished? Then I compare answers to see if there is consistency. If there isn't consistency, it is generally because no vision exists or the vision is not being clearly communicated. Churches like this cannot get moving because even the first spark plug has not fired and the culture remains unmoved.

2. Is our culture healthy and alive?

As a team, we evaluate our culture in all aspects of ministry. This is when we use an evaluation we call the "water line." We ask ourselves if the church ministries and program that we currently have in place are helpful and positively impacting our culture.

I remember a few years back, during the build up of the Y2K scare, there was heaviness on our people due to all the doomsayers' predictions. After analyzing the situation we decided our culture needed some lightening up; we needed to experience joy and infuse our culture with laughter. As a result, we developed a series of silly videos using our staff pastors. We showed these clips at the announcement times during our weekend services. People laughed so hard it brought tears to their eyes and we saw the heaviness lifted. Our analysis had been right and our strategy worked to bring relief to our culture. It was the right plan for that specific season of our church. Although showing funny videos can be counterproductive when poorly timed, that particular strategy worked because we knew what our culture needed at that moment.

Another significant discovery we have made is the blind spot to the power of corporate culture. Time and again we have found that churches have not instilled purposeful change in their culture for years. Culture must continually be addressed for sustained growth to occur.

3. Is our present structure adequate, or is it inhibiting the culture from achieving the vision?

As a team, we determine if our leadership infrastructure is large enough to take the church to a new level of effectiveness. Is our leadership infrastructure adequate for new growth? Do we need to expand facilities or add services? We evaluate our structure and organization to make sure it is properly serving the rest of the synergy cycle. I can tell you from years of experience that structure must always be viewed as a work in progress.

After a time of progression, we begin another revolution on the synergy cycle of vision, culture and structure. As a leader

adopts this style of synergistic leadership, it is importan'
remember a few points:

- For the church to advance, this momentum can never stop.
- The growth and progression of vision, culture, and structure must be in a constant state of change.
- Even vision is not meant to be static; it must be refined,
developed, and restated as the church matures.
- Culture and structure must always be flexible; their ever-
changing development will influence the degree to which the
church can move ahead.

4. Is your leadership team maturing with the changing culture?

To facilitate momentum as a church grows, the roles of staff
members need to change, especially those of the senior pastor. In
the beginning stages of a church, the pastor and his wife do it all
– counseling, weddings, funerals, leading the small groups, even
running the nursery! But as the church progresses, the pastor
must hand off responsibilities to other competent leaders. This
will result in a change of culture and may be hard for people who
always expect a direct line to the senior pastor. Some will happily
embrace the change in structure, granting the pastor the freedom
to take on new roles, even though it means adjusting their culture. Others will find these changes difficult and may eventually

leave the church, seeking the personal attention that they were accustomed to receiving.

It is natural as a church grows for the senior pastor to relate less with the individual church members and more with his expanding leadership team. Clearly, there are small church cultures and large church cultures, with growing pains through the phases in between. A pastor of a 100-member church cannot just wake up one day and begin to act like a pastor of 1,000.

I liken this synergy concept to building a great bonfire. It would never work to light a match and throw a log on it in hopes of having a roaring fire. Instead, the church planter gathers tinder and very small kindling into a pile and gingerly puts a match to it. He shelters it and protects it as the flame begins to catch. When he is confident that the fire is beginning to burn, he adds small sticks until heat begins to generate. Then he adds larger sticks until the fire is ready to ignite a good-sized log. Larger logs are finally piled on until a massive fire is roaring, one that will keep burning even if it begins to rain.

But consider a pastor who tries to maintain a fire with tinder and kindling, never adding the larger logs to the fire. His fire will demand his attention day and night until he is worn out. A pastor must feed his church's fire with different gifts as the momentum of the work grows. A pastor of a large church rarely does weddings, counseling, and many of the tasks that he had to do in the early phases of the church. Over time, he puts his energy into the right people who are often more gifted for these roles.

These changes in structure and transitions in culture must be gradual but constant. Each time the church goes around the synergy cycle and the culture is visited, the roles of key leaders must be reevaluated and the structure adjusted appropriately.

I remember one time when we were struggling to break a growth barrier, and I took my organizational chart to John Wimber. I asked if he could see a bottleneck in our structure that was holding us back. As I rolled out this long scroll of paper before him, he took a quick glance and simply said, "Go home and fix your nursery." I did just that, and the church grew. It is often a good idea to have an objective and experienced pair of eyes to take a constructive look at what you are doing. Often they can see the deficits or barriers that you cannot.

Another structural weakness is commonly found in the eldership of a church. We often discover that, in most stagnated churches, the elders aren't "elding." That is to say, the elders are not functioning as leaders of leaders; they are not aggressively leading the way in developing new ministry. This can be a painful reality to the senior pastor, though it is an issue that can be rectified.

LEADERSHIP 401 SEMINARS

For churches that are ready and willing to promote cultural and structural change, we periodically host a Leadership 401 seminar at Vineyard Boise. This seminar is for church leadership teams who recognize their need to discover invisible barriers that are inhibiting growth. We invite only those teams who are accompanied by the senior pastor and bring at least three eldership-level leaders. I have found that leadership seminars are only truly productive when you are dealing with the people who can promote major change.

We ask the teams to bring three forms of evaluation with them (provided for them in advance to complete), as well as their church's vision statement. We also request them to bring a copy of their church by-laws and their annual budget. (If you want to know what a church values, just look at how they spend their money.) We have also discovered that most churches have not revised or consulted their by-laws since the day of incorporation.

The 401 seminar (www.revolutionaryleadership-book.com for details) is conducted over three days, teaching the synergy principles, and challenging each team to discern strengths and weakness in each element. We help them discover how they can bring slow, methodical changes in the work they are doing. This will enable them to break down barriers so that growth can be re-stimulated.

FINAL STATEMENTS

I encourage you to never stop going around the synergy cycle and never neglect an annual evaluation – this will ensure that your church will grow and develop year after year. Change is often like the hour hand on a clock, it seems like nothing is happening but one day you will look up and realize that your church is moving once again.

Synergetic leadership will make your church grow in breadth and depth, causing a swirl of charismatic life – and like a giant magnet, it will begin to attract, pull in, and impact the community that it endeavors to change.

I believe by applying these principles, you will be able to evaluate your church and see the strengths and weaknesses. It is my sincere hope that this will help you discover what the Lord is blessing, enabling you to invest your passion and energy in fulfilling your vision.

I pray the Lord will empower and energize you to once again embrace the dreams that led you to begin your leadership journey – giving you new tools to grow the church and ministry He has put in your heart to build.

God's Relentless Pursuit: Discovering His Heart for Humanity
by Phil Strout
retail price: $14.95

Have you ever considered that instead of us chasing God, He is actually the One chasing us? In his book, author Phil Strout explores God's mission on earth and how His people join in His mission: to draw people into relationship with Him. Many common ideas and notions regarding our role in pursuing God are challenged as we discover the truth about what God is doing in and around us, both across the street and across the oceans.

Sample chapters and book are available for purchase at: www.ampelonpublishing.com

Passionate Pursuit: Discovering the Heart of Christ
by Jason Chatraw
retail price: $9.95

Do you want to experience a greater intimacy in the time you spend with God? If so, the devotional *Passionate Pursuit* helps set you on the right path. We must know that our relationship with God is a journey, not a quick trip. And being equipped for the journey will make it more fun and exciting.

Sample chapters and book are available for purchase at: www.ampelonpublishing.com